Remnants of War

Retracing the sites of conflict and reconciliation

Remnants of War

Retracing the Sites of Conflict and Reconciliation

Edited by

Paul Skrebels

Contributors

Peter Bishop, Richard Chew, John Cokley, Kerry Green, Sue Page, William Park, Paul Skrebels, Nigel Starck, Claire Woods

LYTHRUM PRESS
Adelaide

First published by
Lythrum Press
PO Box 243 Rundle Mall
Adelaide
South Australia 5000

in association with the University of South Australia

First published November 2009

Typeset by Michael Deves, Lythrum Press
Printed and bound by Griffin Digital

ISBN 978 1 921013 24 9

Acknowledgements
Judith Timoney for editorial work and project assistance
Nigel Starck for cover photographs

Contents

Introduction

This collection represents the second offering from the University of South Australia's Narratives of War research group. A number of contributors to the first monograph, *Writings of War* (Woods & Timoney 2008), have also written chapters for this one, but the focus here is markedly different. Here in *Remnants of War* the emphasis is firmly on the theme of place in relation to issues of conflict and reconciliation, and so to some extent is in keeping with current trends in historical research and writing. James Boyce, for example, in his ground-breaking and highly acclaimed study of the European settlement of Tasmania, describes his work as 'an environmental history': 'not because it explains how convict settlers changed the environment but because its primary interest is how the environment changed *them*' (Boyce 2008, p. 11). Many other recent works are based on the same premise, and no doubt many more to come will be informed by their writers' willingness to don, in Peter Stanley's words, 'a stout pair of boots' and wander around their respective locations.[1]

Remnants of War, however, is not a work of history, or rather, not a work of history only. For a start, its chapters are as much concerned with the present as with the past, and certainly with understanding the relationship between the two. Next, none of its contributors are professional historians in the strict sense of the term, even if most of us share a love of researching and writing about the past. Even so, there is little question that each of the studies presented here deals with the influence of specific places on both historical and present-day actors and events. More to the point, though, is the effect coming into actual physical contact with sites of significance has had on the writers themselves. This is because each chapter is informed by direct experience of the places under discussion; all the writers have made the effort, in one form or other, to visit and explore the 'settings' central to their particular research interests.

As reading each chapter will reveal, the results have been twofold. First, the places tend to move from 'mere' setting to centre-stage; each has become a focus of attention and analysis in itself, as a major participant in the historical, social and cultural processes under consideration. Second is the degree to which 'being there' has provided each writer with fresh eyes with which to see—literally, to 're-view'—their subjects, and to reflect more purposefully on the interaction between people, events and places. If revisionism is one of the current buzz-words in historical and other studies in the humanities and social sciences, then surely the pieces in this collection demonstrate just how essential a strong sense of place can be to revising, if not overturning, the preconceptions and self-imposed disciplinary constraints that limit our understanding of the world.

As a way of illustrating the interdisciplinary and eclectic approaches taken in this collection, there is a word that crops up in several chapters that requires some explanation. Working quite independently of each other, at least three of the writers here (one of them me) have used the term 'palimpsest' in referring to some aspect of the landscape they're dealing with. It originally meant 'parchment or other material from which the original writing has been erased to make room for another record' (*Concise English Dictionary* 1984, p. 818), such materials being so scarce and expensive—not to mention durable—that they were routinely scraped clean and rewritten on. Literary critics have picked up on the physical characteristic of palimpsests, to retain visible traces of earlier texts beneath and alongside the existing text, as an allegory for the inherent intertextuality of all texts.[2] The propensity for contributors to this collection to use the term in their examinations of places attests not only to their own cross-disciplinary methods, but also to their willingness to regard landscapes, memorials and other sites, justifiably, as texts in their own right, capable of being read and interpreted as readily as anything written, filmed, photographed or otherwise 'mediated'. In other words, places have layers of meaning which can be discovered and analysed; *Remnants of War* thus proposes a form of archaeology without the actual digging.

So it is in this spirit of subjecting sites of conflict and reconciliation to a wide range of critical perspectives that Peter Bishop's chapter, 'Playing in the wreckage', opens the collection. In one of only two pieces here dealing with actual battlefield locations[3]—which he says are particularly potent 'memoryscapes', capable of attracting 'pilgrims' of many kinds and age-groups—Peter adopts various points of view and posits several crucial questions as he leads his family on a recreational and educational tour of significant WW2 sites: in Singapore, Italy, London, and Normandy and Dunkirk in France. Peter's trip is inspired partly by wishing to retrace the experiences of his father who served in the British forces in North Africa and Italy and of his mother during the various phases of the London Blitz. But he also draws inspiration for his quest from the various screen representations of the D-Day landings in Normandy, in cinema, TV, and in video and computer game form. He is thus able to raise some key generational and cultural issues, such as how young people now at least twice-removed from the experience of WW2 respond to such sites; whether young German visitors are 'subject to a different story' from the dominant narrative that casts their nation as the 'baddies'; and the appropriateness or otherwise of the methods employed by contemporary museology that embrace both education and entertainment in commemorating battlefield sites. Ultimately Peter concludes that memorialisation and reconciliation are complex and on-going processes which, in a world of increasingly multicultural societies, need to open up entry points for contemporary and future generations.

Peter's discussion of the Italian leg of his trip, where he acknowledges the 'substantial silences about WW2 in postwar Italian culture', provides a springboard for my own chapter, 'Furphies, follies and fugitives'. Here I deal with my own recent visit to Italy to follow the prisoner-of-war career of English author Dan Billany. He and fellow

POW David Dowie wrote a remarkable account—part memoir, part novel—of their experiences which, even though they both disappeared without trace following the Italian Armistice in September 1943, was published in 1949 as *The Cage*. I managed to reach two of their three prison camps, the much-renovated castle at Rezzanello, and the former orphanage, now district hospital, at Fontanellato. I use extracts from both *The Cage* and Billany's letters to his family to provide an insight into life in both places, while at the same time exploring how the peculiarities of each influenced the subject matter and style of their literary work. At the same time I managed to see that while the 'silences' mentioned by Peter certainly persist in some places, in others the spirit of memorialisation and reconciliation is promoted and maintained.

The theme of prison camps points us in the direction of the next two chapters. Nigel Starck's 'Putting away childish things' involves his journeys to five sites featured in the WW2 and Cold War literature he read in his younger days: Colditz Castle, Anne Frank's house in Amsterdam, Dachau concentration camp, the Berlin Wall, and the Stasi Museum in Leipzig. His quest, to see if the reality still matches the special qualities each place is endowed with in the literature. Nigel cross-references his own witty and erudite observations with passages from these works, and reveals that in some cases there are enough traces left to evoke something of their original power, albeit not without a certain amount of help from the museologist's craft. Not so others, however, which, no matter how hard their curators may try, retain none of the *frisson* of the books in which they featured so prominently. Some sites, he comes to realise, can only live on in the imagination.

Nigel's comment on Dachau, that 'German schoolchildren ... are permitted to learn—without revisionism—the excesses of their nation's past', leads inexorably to Sue Page's chapter, 'We're not German', a disturbing and heartfelt account of Austria's contrasting unwillingness to acknowledge its part in the those same Nazi excesses. Sue's work was inspired by her finding little in the way of memorials in Austria to that period, and an all too frequently dismissive attitude to it among its people. She raises the concept of 'traumascapes' as a variant of memoryscapes, and realises that the apparently generally accepted notion that these should be marked and remembered is in fact culturally determined and by no means universally upheld. Austria, she finds, is a 'look-away society' with a culture of forgetting. In response, she visits one of its few memorial sites to the Holocaust, the concentration camp of Mauthausen, and gives us a harrowing and eloquent account of her experiences as a 'nonwitness'—a term that helps define herself as more than a casual tourist. The experience, she maintains, was not simply vicarious, and in a statement that could stand as the motto for this whole collection, she says, 'I can never visit the time; I can visit the place.'

Kerry Green's chapter, 'Power in paradise', is the first in a group of pieces that brings this field of research home, as it were, and is a tribute to the part played by Cairns and the North Queensland area in the war against Japan from 1941 to 1945. This was a crucial zone in Australia's war effort, not only because of its proximity to the South-West Pacific theatre of war, but because its climate and ecology made it a perfect training ground for troops about to embark for operations in that theatre. Kerry's chapter is a journey around that area, taking note of the traces of the hundreds of thousands of Australian and American troops who passed through it, but also of the more far-reaching consequences such as the drained swamps and the wharves built to sustain the war effort. Of special note is the homage Kerry pays to local historian Vera Bradley and others like her, who are capable of providing us with unique and deeper insights into the significance of particular places in the scheme of things.

The notion of traces is of particular importance to Claire Woods' chapter, 'A biography of the Dinkums'. Claire is working with me on a project that will effectively reinvent and re-present the WW1 unit history of the South Australian 27th Battalion AIF (nicknamed 'The

Dinkums'), *The Blue and Brown Diamond*, originally published in 1921, in digital form for modern readers and researchers. Claire has more than a passing interest in the subject; her father Stan was an officer in the unit, a Military Cross winner in 1917, and one of the editorial committee that oversaw the production of the original battalion history. As part of our research into the formation of the unit, Claire has visited and followed the progress of the 27th into what was once the Mitcham Army Camp, but transformed in the 1930s into the Adelaide suburb of Colonel Light Gardens. Claire does this by skilfully adopting the role of the *flâneur*, promulgated by the great cultural historian Walter Benjamin (via Charles Beaudelaire), to stroll about the streets and pathways of the former campsite in order to evoke an ethnography of the 27th's—and by extension every other unit's—experiences at Mitcham during WW1. And, she maintains, while it may seem impossible to re-establish a link between past and present when not only the participants have passed on, but the place itself has been razed and ploughed into oblivion, this can be achieved in virtual form by the careful gathering and re-presenting of the traces left behind: the photos, maps, diaries and other documents, that will once more allow an apparently unremarkable corner of a city to tell its story of the experiences of these men to subsequent generations.

William Park and John Cokley's chapter, 'Counting on archives', is a noteworthy contribution to this collection for several reasons. First, it is the only 'guest' contribution to what is otherwise an all-Narratives of War group effort. Claire Woods and I heard Bill and John present a version of it to a conference in Brisbane, were hugely impressed by the quality and originality of the research and findings, and wanted to provide them with a way of making it more widely recognised as such. Second—despite one's awareness in this era of equal opportunity that it shouldn't be remarked upon—Bill Park is, at the time of writing, eighty-nine years old and only recently a graduate of the University of Queensland's Master of Philosophy program. Thus, third, even though this is the only chapter not dealing with place as a physical entity, Bill most definitely was 'there' in Queensland at the time he describes, and is himself a subject of the *World War 2 Nominal Roll* his and John's chapter analyses and criticises. Besides, Bill's idea sprang from his recognition that the Honour Roll board at Queensland Uni, a place of which he has been a part in various guises since 1939, was not an accurate reflection of the service of its alumni. Fourth, the *Nominal Roll* constitutes the kind of virtual place advocated by Claire in her chapter as a way of bridging the gap between past and present, and which researchers can visit as surely as any real library or archive. The concern that he and John Cokley, who was his thesis supervisor, have is that the resource be an accurate record, and both have charted in detailed and precise form how that can and should be achieved.

If importance and originality are criteria by which to judge contributions to this collection, then surely the closing chapter, Richard Chew's 'Viridiana: Mostar 2004' fits the bill in spades. Richard is a music teacher and current PhD student at the University of South Australia, and a very gifted composer into the bargain. His chapter brings the discussion of conflict and reconciliation up to date by dealing with the more recent war in Bosnia fought on ethnic lines as part of the break-up of the former nation of Yugoslavia. In it he describes the writing of a commissioned piece, an oratorio called *Stari Most*, celebrating the rebuilding of the bridge at Mostar, which despite its historical and cultural importance was callously destroyed by Croatian artillery fire in 1993. Richard uses a combination of journal-style entries and a detailed analysis of the research and writing involved in the composition process to explain how he worked with the words of librettist Peter Cann, and to describe the visit he actually made to Mostar in order to gain a clearer sense of his subject matter. He manages to lay bare the inner motivations of a work that ultimately, and in keeping with the aims of this collection as a whole, Richard says left him 'with a belief in the possibility of hope in the face of overwhelming odds'.[4]

Yet another Richard, Richard Holmes, has been hailed 'as the pioneer of a new way of doing biography' through a technique he calls 'footstepping': 'Following in the tracks of his subjects, warming their trails with the breath of sympathetic imagination, he finds he can better understand and imagine them' (Slattery 2008). We in the Narratives of War research group offer our readers this collection of pieces in the same spirit of footstepping through the significant sites of our research and for exactly the same reasons. While we hope that you are presented with similar opportunities, we are sure that you will find the experiences presented here, if of necessity vicarious ones, no less interesting and informative.

Paul Skrebels
Adelaide, October 2009

Notes

1 There is also a school of environmental history dealing with how humans have affected the landscape, which is not what is being referred to here. Another noteworthy example of Boyce's approach to environmental history is Grace Karskens' new version of the founding of Sydney (2009). Peter Stanley (2008) uses the 'boots' phrase as the title for his book about walking the battlefields where Australians fought, and has applied the method to his studies of Quinn's Post (2005) and Mont St Quentin (2009).

2 A key figure in this regard is Gérard Genette (1997, orig. 1982), whose study, principally of parodies, satires and pastiches, sets out to establish the many relationships between a text and its antecedents.

3 The other is Richard Chew's story of his visit to Mostar and the composition of his musical tribute to the rebuilding of its famous bridge, which closes this collection.

4 As a fitting postscript, it should be pointed out that *Stari Most* that was given a full-blown performance—by all accounts to great effect—in Salisbury Cathedral in the UK in October 2008.

References

Boyce, J 2008, *Van Diemen's Land*, Black Inc, Melbourne.

The Concise English Dictionary 1984, Cassell/Omega, Ware.

Genette, G 1997, *Palimpsests: Literature in the second degree*, orig 1982, trans C Newman & C Doubinsky, University of Nebraska, Lincoln.

Karskens, G 2009, *The colony: A history of early Sydney*, Allen & Unwin, Crows Nest, NSW.

Slattery, L 2008, 'In the footsteps of past masters', *Australian*, 10 September, viewed 17 April 2009, < http://www.theaustralian.news.com.au/story/0,25197,24320202-12332,00.html>.

Stanley, P 2005, *Quinn's Post: Anzac, Gallipoli*, Allen & Unwin, Crows Nest, NSW.

Stanley, P 2008, *A stout pair of boots: A guide to exploring Australia's battlefields*, Allen & Unwin, Crows Nest, NSW.

Stanley, P 2009, *Men of Mont St Quentin: Between victory and death*, Scribe, Melbourne.

Woods, C & Timoney, J, eds 2008, *Writings of war*, Lythrum Press, Adelaide.

Chapter 1

Playing in the wreckage: A family visit to the site of D-Day and other WW2 battlefields

Peter Bishop
University of South Australia

Introduction: family background

Between May and July 2008 I travelled with my wife, eighteen-year-old daughter and two sons aged eleven and sixteen, to Singapore, France, Italy and the UK to visit various battle sites connected with WW2. Our itinerary included locations in Singapore; various places where fighting occurred in Italy, especially Salerno and Cassino; the Imperial War Museum and some sites of the bombing in London; sites in France, such as around the Dunkirk region and, in particular, the D-Day battlefields in Normandy.

With war on the immediate horizon my father, a Londoner, almost thirty years old and married, had volunteered and, as a dispatch rider in the Signals Corps was sent with the small BEF (British Expeditionary Force) to Northern France. He was subsequently evacuated in desperate conditions from the beaches of Dunkirk. Then, after three years in North Africa with the 8th Army he was part of the British contingent which, with the mainly American force, fought their way ashore at Salerno in Southern Italy. One of his younger brothers was wounded at Cassino and my dad told stories about visiting him there in hospital. Although she had lost many friends and suffered great hardships on the home front, including damage to her house, my mother had survived the Blitz in London while my dad was overseas. Later in the war she had also survived the bombardment by V1 rockets and V2 missiles, but only just. Our house along with several others had been completely destroyed by a V1 and a few months later a V2 had destroyed another section of the street. Fortunately, my mum and brother (then just a toddler) and my uncle, an emotionally scarred veteran of Gallipoli, and my grandmother were not at home when the rocket destroyed half the street and killed many of her neighbours. In my early years, I had played among the rubble-strewn bomb sites. On a previous visit to London I had taken my very elderly parents to the Imperial War Museum's themed 'Blitz Experience', much to my mother's satisfaction, as she felt insufficient recognition had been given to the long periods when the Home Front had been the front line. The prime focus of our visit to London was the street where our house was bombed and I was born, plus the Imperial War Museum, particularly the 'Blitz Experience'.

The D-Day sites were therefore unique for me and my family. Unlike Singapore, there are no significant Australian associations with the Normandy landings. It is not a site on the landscape of Australian national identity-formation. Also, unlike the sites in London, Italy and in Northern France around Dunkirk, those in Normandy had no family associations.

The D-Day landscape today

The D-Day region is one of the most complex and densely memorialised battle regions of WW2. It is comprehensively saturated with every conceivable signifier of the events that spanned from D-Day itself through the months that followed. The logistics of the actual assault and subsequent battles dictates the immediate physical area: the coast from Cherbourg to that directly north of Caen—a distance of approximately 100 kms. It then goes inland some fifty-plus kms from St Lo, Bayeux and Caen. The markers include numerous museums of various size, complexity and official-ness; a host of heritage/information markers; cemeteries; preserved parts of the German defences, the Atlantic Wall; preserved scars of the battle—from destroyed bunkers to shell holes made by the bombardment from Allied warships and aircraft; various shops selling mementos and even original items—uniforms, weapons, and any of the vast paraphernalia of that war; recreations of key parts of

Figure 1 Colleville sur Mer, Normandy, June 2008 (author's photo)

the German defences; numerous tanks and artillery-pieces parked at significant places; and the remains of the Mulberry artificial harbour. There are a multitude of possible tours on offer. The complete range of educational, representational and entertainment resources that are available to contemporary museology are deployed across the whole landscape. (See Figure 1)

Battlefield memoryscapes

The D-Day sites form what has come to be called a memoryscape (Gough 2004). Muzaini and Yeoh put it succinctly: 'Collective memory is commonly spatialized through the material and symbolic shaping of memoryscapes (or memorial landscapes)' (2005, p. 345). Similarly, Gough, commenting on the 16.5 hectares of preserved WW1 battlefield that forms the Beaumont Hamel Newfoundland Memorial on the Somme, describes the site as a 'dramaturgical space where terrain has been rearranged to create a sequence of spatial and timed narratives' (2004, p. 248). He cites a description of 'the memorial-strewn sites of the US Civil War as "landscapes of accretion", stratified by layer upon layer of markers, statuary, beacons and military ordnance which require careful excavation'(2004, p. 249).

There is a profound difference between a memorial which is located far from the site of battle and one located at the site itself. In fact just the site alone, without any commemorative enhancement can have a fundamental imaginative power. Richard Holmes, commenting on a visit to the D-Day sites, puts it simply: 'There is a haunting quality to battlefields' (cited in Bougaardt 2004, p. 6). As Gough suggests,

> When compared to transient phenomena and ill-considered monuments, certain geographical locations appear to be able to offer a sense of legitimate permanence that draws pilgrims to sites that "place" or "contain" the memory of overwhelming events. (2004, p. 237)

He continues: 'preserved battlefield sites can help to concretize the experience of war and evoke profound reflections' (2004, p. 238).

There are important differences, as well as overlaps, 'between sites of battle, sites of memory and sites of mourning' (Winter, cited in Gough 2004, p. 237). The Normandy memoryscape has all three.

The other key aspect of the landscape, one which complements the compelling *mise-en-scène* constructed within the actual physical landscape, is the virtual world of D-Day. This is particularly crucial for evoking and sustaining the interest of young people. As with many battlegrounds any visit to the physical place is often accompanied, preceded and followed by an encounter with a thick, multi-dimensional narrative and visual contextualisation that enframes the direct experience of the place itself. In her study of an Australian TV mini-series *Changi*, about the notorious WW2 Japanese prisoner-of-war camp in Singapore, Paula Hamilton mobilises the notion of 'prosthetic memory' to discuss the way in which, as a result of electronic media, 'people are able to take on memories of a past to which they have no historical or geographical connection, and with people whom they don't know' (2009, pp. 138-9). In most contemporary societies public memory and mass media are totally interconnected. Importantly, it is argued that film and TV 'disturbs as many narratives as it confirms' (Winter, cited in Hamilton 2009, p. 145).

Prior to our visit, for example, we had all seen the film *Saving Private Ryan* and it had become a key text for all of us. We are not alone in giving this kind of significance to the film. It has replaced *The Longest Day* as the seminal contemporary cinematic experience of D-Day and has become a touchstone of combat verité on D-Day (for example, Bougaardt 2004, p. 10). Browsing various books and, especially, computer, play station and video action games based on D-Day (such as *The Band of Brothers*; *Brothers in Arms; Medal of Honour; Call of Duty*), had created a landscape of expectation in our family. Even the film *Charlotte Gray* had drawn everyone into the world of women and the French Resistance. Some of the brochures issued at D-Day commemorative sites explicitly established cross-links with the mediascape. For example, the brochure from *Dead Man's Corner Museum* at Saint-Come-du-Mont, which memorialises the American soldiers of the 101st Airborne, carries the acknowledgement: 'In partnership with Brothers in Arms', accompanied by a frame from the playstation/computer game.

Contested readings, contested sites

There is considerable literature, both analytical and of a personally descriptive nature, about visits to battlefields (for example, Hutchison 2006; Woods 1994; Davies 2008; Bouugaardt 2004). The construction of battlefield monuments, the design of heritage centres and the preservation of landscapes are rarely without controversy. Michael Heffernan, for example, gives a detailed analysis of the vigorous and contentious debates in Britain that began even as WW1 was still going on, debates which continued for many years after the war's conclusion, over how to memorialise the battlefields (1995). In other words these sites rarely just spring into existence. Post-conflict, they evolve and change. Similarly, the types of traveller, the reasons for and type of the journey, change over the years. Combatants grow old and pass on. Sites such as Kokoda can suddenly loom large and shift in their significance while others may just fade away.

Paul Gough suggests that, 'commemoration is always an act of evaluation, judgement and "speaking"' and that 'it is neither possible nor desirable to insist on a single, objective and authoritative reading of any place or historic monument' (2004, p. 236). He continues: 'Battlefield markers and signage lend authority to a particular reading of the space. Memory is reassigned and controlled' (2004, p. 251). Rather than a single way of reading:

> it is more realistic to consider the semiotic of memoryscapes as a 'palimpsest of overlapping multi-vocal landscapes' each seeking to defend—discursively and materially—its own historical memory as the bone fide one. (Saunders, cited in Muzaini & Yeoh 2005, p. 346)

Even the actuality of the physical landscape can be contentious. Muzaini and Yeoh, discussing the WW2 battlefield memorial to the Malay Regiment at Bukit Changdu in Singapore, report controversies and confusions about where the actual battle took place and how this uncertainty undermines the symbolic veracity of commemoration for some visitors (2005). As will be shown in the case of D-Day commemorations, such contestations can continue long after the conflict as crucial complex identities, both historical and contemporary, are renegotiated.

Generational questions

At one point while we were exploring the ruined gun emplacements along the Normandy coast, some with guns still intact and signs of D-Day shell-fire etched into both the concrete and the earth, we noticed a large group of teenage boys and girls, quietly laughing and joking with each other, beginning to catch us up. They looked like a high school outing and they were enjoying themselves. It wasn't particularly busy so we decided to hang around and let them pass. My daughter and teenage son both cast interested glances at these new arrivals, after all we had been on the road for a long time and interaction with kids of their own age had been rare. They'd quite liked observing how European kids their own age looked and behaved, what they were wearing and what country they came from. When we heard them chatting away in German it provoked curiosity and reflection about why they had come to these sites. It also made me wonder why their presence surprised us. The dominant narrative of D-Day 'country' that had been built up through the memoryscape projected a kind of pure battlefield told almost totally from the perspective of one side and which, while complex in details, was basically contained within a very simplistic frame. There was a lack of narrative contestation. The sheer physical actuality of the sites reinforced this dominant narrative. Pointing to D-Day, along with other sites of battles, Gough writes:

> In each place the moral resonance of the site itself is seen as paramount. Ditches, mounds, ruins and apparently barren tracts have been maintained because they are seen as 'historical traces' which have an authority that now eclipses the untenable artifice of the commemorative object. (2004, p. 237)

The major direction taken by our reflections was prompted by my teenage children who asked a crucial question: Why were these German teenagers here? By this they meant, what were *their* reasons for visiting this place? What kind of place were *they* seeing? What was *their* dominant story of D-Day? Everything in the media and in the memorialised landscape overwhelmingly cast the Germans as the baddies, not demonised in a stereotypical way but as the oppressive occupiers of France and of Europe as a whole. It seemed as if most of the world celebrated the landings as a huge blow for freedom. How did these teenagers respond to this? Were they subject to a different story? If so where was it to be found? There had been very little, if any indication of attempted reconciliation in the media or landscape. It was as if time alone had been left to heal any wounds. Our family discussion moved on to how it would be to grow up three or more generations after a war in which not only was your country on the losing side but which was so universally condemned as being grossly in the wrong?

We had just been to various battle sites in Italy so we also started puzzling over the legacy of the war in which Italy started on Germany's side (indeed my Dad, their grandad, spent many years fighting them in North Africa and even briefly in Italy itself). The Italian government then surrendered and switched sides, with Italy becoming torn apart by a complex and very nasty mix of civil war, war of resistance against the Germans who, angry at the betrayal by their former allies, treated the Italian population quite cruelly, and continued fighting against the Allies by Italian fascist forces. At the same time Italian civilians caught in a protracted and highly intense conflict between the Germans and the Allies, suffered heavily. To make matters worse, the Allied campaign in Italy, despite huge battles and appalling casualties, was treated as a sideshow to the invasion being planned for France. Even the celebration over the conquest/ liberation of Rome on 5 June 1944, which was the first Axis capital city to fall, was immediately overshadowed the very next day by the events in Normandy. No wonder memorialisation is sparse and muted.
In postwar accounts by the old Allied countries there is a strange absence about the Italians and about the Allied campaign in Italy. The substantial silences about the WW2 in postwar Italian culture are conspicuous. Italian movies that address WW2, for example, from the realist classics of the immediate postwar to contemporary ones, emphasise either a reluctance about fighting alongside the Germans or detail Italians actually fighting against them. Most Italians seem represented as either victims or partisans. With few exceptions there is a lack of WW2 memorials in battlefield Italy. Unlike the Atlantic wall of D-Day, there has been an almost complete erasure of the

extraordinary series of German defensive lines running from coast to coast up the entire length of Italy (Short 2006). We mused on this as we stood around the ruined bunkers of D-Day listening to the German teenagers chatting. How do contemporary Italian teenagers experience the history of Italy's involvement in the war? What are the narratives to which they are exposed?

After our encounter with the German youth our reflections, or at least mine, took off in two other directions. One of these concerned the difference between clearly marked, deliberately memorialised battle sites and the far more numerous ones that have no markers, no commemorative indicators. Commenting on the Blitz, for example, the German bombing of British cities in 1940/1, John Ray criticises the fact that 'no suitable national memorial exists to the 60,000 civilians' who were killed let alone the vast numbers seriously wounded during WW2 in Britain (1998, p.12). We had also previously visited the site of the WW2 landings at Salerno in Italy, where we had swum and enjoyed ourselves on the beaches next to the famous archaeological site of Paestum, with its extraordinarily intact Greek-Roman remains. This was also the site that defined the southern end of the landing beaches where the American's had fought their way ashore. There were no markers to commemorate this event—the first major amphibious landing on occupied mainland Europe and an important precursor to the D-Day assault. The fighting here had been desperate.

At this point another train of reflection took off: what is the appropriate protocol or decorum when visiting such sites of battle? So, is laughing appropriate? By 'us'? By 'them'? The laughing and playing around by the German youth wasn't loud and after all, they weren't at some inscribed solemn marker, a conspicuous shrine or memorial, nor were they at a cemetery. It is a reminder that battlefield memoryscapes are not homogeneous. They are comprised of micro-sites of varying intensity at which various protocols can and do co-exist. The German youth were climbing in and over concrete gun emplacements in much the same way that we had just a few moments before. They were enjoying themselves. Is one supposed to enjoy oneself at a commemorated battlefield site, especially if your recent ancestors and relatives were almost universally agreed to be the bad guys? Are WW2 and WW1 sites different to others that came earlier? If so, why? How close in time or just in space to the historical markers does one have to be before laughing becomes a question? In what ways does one's nationality, ethnicity, gender or age matter?

It was early summer at the D-Day beaches when we visited, still a bit cold and rainy but many children and families were playing, swimming and windsurfing along beaches. Sections of the vast artificial harbour, so crucial to the invasion, still remained just offshore with young people climbing on them. I wondered how many remains of combatants lay beneath the sand on the seabed. Was this a vast unmarked war grave? It has been reported that the landing beaches were reopened to holidaymakers barely a year after the invasion, with dangerous areas conspicuously signposted and warnings issued (Clout 2009, p. 173). Similarly, laughing was of course common in the un-memorialised post-blitzed street where I was born and where many civilians died. The numerous local bomb sites were used as playgrounds. We mucked around with various old paraphernalia such as tin hats and gas masks. The air raid shelters, both large public ones and small private ones in back gardens, were great for games as were the concrete bunkers along the English south-east coast. Listening to my mother's tales of the Blitz and looking at the many signs of that struggle around our neighbourhood, I often wondered if German airmen, (and their children or grandchildren) came to London to revisit their battle sites?

After any battle a complex process of physical, social and personal reconstruction must occur. As Richard Holmes puts it, having fought their way ashore on D-Day, 'soon the invaders met civilians, for this battlefield was their home' (cited in Bougaardt 2004, p. 6). Hugh Clout's detailed study of the labour to repair Lower Normandy after the landings at Utah Beach and after the subsequent fighting shows how long, complicated and painful was this process (2009). Complex strands of reconciliation are key aspects of this reconstruction, (e.g. between Allies/Axis; combatants/ civilians; resistance fighters/ collaborators; even between various Allied nationalities). While at its most intense, painful and fraught immediately post-conflict, reconciliation needs to be embedded into the narratives about that conflict and into its memorialisation. Reconciliation is not a one-time event but an ongoing, ever-changing process. Key aspects of the memoryscape need to be constantly adapted to meet different historical circumstances and audiences.

Serious tourists in the memory theatre

Richard Holmes insists that

> War walks are indispensible to military history, for painstaking map study never quite summons up the right image. And there are fragments of 'microterrain' which spring out of the ground itself. (cited in Bougaardt 2004, p. 6)

He continues: 'visiting battlefields touches heart as well as head'. However, whether for the purposes of intellectually confirming historical details or for encouraging emotional empathy, there is much controversy about attempts to orchestrate visitors' experiences of battlefields through various on-site devices. In particular, the idea that a visit to a battle site should be akin to entertainment seems anathema to some. As Gough points out: 'Many commentators despise the form of vicarious entertainment' (2004, p. 249). This echoes many criticisms of contemporary museological technologies which emphasise entertainment, contrasting it with serious education (Wright 1985; Lowenthal 1985; Vergo 1989).

On the other hand, Raphael Samuel is particularly forgiving, even appreciative, of even fairly tangential and entertaining opportunities to explore history, such as secondhand shops or historical re-enactments, or period films (1994). He argues that any liberties taken with historical accuracy are often compensated for by the evocation of a sense of historical imagination. This is especially important when it comes to direct contact with physical actuality. To this extent the many shops located around the various D-Day sites, whether selling reproductions or original artefacts, educational material or souvenirs, as well as the ruined bunkers and bombarded landscape, assume particular significance within a kind of historical pedagogy (1994, pp. 274ff). Samuel insists upon this important role, especially for young people, far removed in time, culture and often in space, from the original event (1994, pp. 177 ff).

Harbison suggests that 'serious tourists' 'help monumentalize the landscapes they pass through', reconstructing events and experiences (cited in Gough 2004, pp. 238–9). But what does it mean to be a serious tourist? I want to consider those serious tourists for whom the experience is entertaining, but not necessarily in a trivial sense. Much so-called entertainment is serious.

The encounter with the young Germans started me thinking about the place of humour in the memorialisation of battle. My family were very familiar, for example, with the well-known BBC TV comedy series *Blackadder Goes Forth*, located in the WW1 trenches. This provided my children with both laughs and insight into the absurdity and insanity of that conflict and of most war. In the final moments of this series the much loved gang of soldiers unexpectedly go over the top only to be greeted by a hail of machine gun fire. It is a profoundly moving moment when the laughing stops and the clowns die. Despite having seen other, more serious and historically 'accurate' films about WW1, when we visited the reconstruction of WW1 trenches at London's Imperial War Museum, it was the *Blackadder* series which they mentioned and which provided my children with the crucial emotional empathy. The list goes on: from the extremely popular *Dad's Army* and *M*A*S*H*, to the extraordinary film *Life is Beautiful*, which attempts the impossible task of creating concentration camp comedy. Even the appalling madness of the more recent conflict and ethnic cleansing in the Balkans is the background of comedy in the film *Life is a Miracle*. Laughter can be profound. A key function of battlefield memoryscapes is educational and many studies confirm that appropriate humour has important pedagogical benefits (Mitchell 2007). Humour can also challenge entrenched narratives.

War and entertainment have gone together in a substantive way since WW2 and probably earlier. Cinema, music, cartoon comics, novels, games, toys, model-building, and comedians have been integral to the pursuance of war not just for the purposes of propaganda, morale and distraction, but as a setting for and topic of entertainment. Humour, of various kinds, has been a part of this. Post-conflict, wars often become a major topic of the entertainment industry and museums have become major players in this (Vergo 1989). As suggested earlier, there is an immense virtual battlefield that not only has a privileged place in popular culture, but is integral to the memorialisation of battles. The geographically located D-Day memoryscape is deliberately integrated with both the virtual memoryscape and the broader entertainment industry. Visitors, particularly families and children, are repeatedly encouraged to enjoy themselves. Respect for those directly involved in the conflict is not diminished because of this and there are clearly defined sites, such as the cemeteries which lie at the extreme edge of the 'entertainment' paradigm and probably, for most people, elude it altogether. Promotion, with its clearly recognised rhetoric of persuasion, proliferates across the D-Day sites. Everything from nationalism to shopping, from themed entertainments to interactive games, tourism to education is duly promoted as reasons to visit the various battle sites in Normandy. The full spectrum of issues and possibilities that accompany advertising and consumerism can be found here (Fowles 1996). For example, the brochure for the Canadian museum for D-Day, the *Centre Juno Beach*, located at Courseulles-sur-Mer, points out that for young visitors there are displays with virtual guides, hands-on presentations and quizzes. It also gives a list of exhibits: Images of D-Day; Canada on the eve of WW2; Mobilisation of Canada; The main Canadian campaigns in Europe leading to VE Day; Personal stories of Canadians from this period; Learn about Canadian culture; Canadian history; Souvenirs from Canada and the Normandy region. This museum has clearly gone beyond a commemoration of D-Day and is being used as an opportunistic platform to also promote Canada.

Cosmopolitan and multi-ethnic encounters

Key conflicts, such as D-Day, are subject to a steady stream of updated studies, each producing new details and interpretations (for example, Beevor 2009). But, in this chapter I'm less interested in increased historical veracity, however important that may be, than about the appropriateness of the memorialisation for contemporary cosmopolitan society, especially for its youth. As Muzaini and Yeoh point out, there are often 'Transnational tensions over memory spaces' and that 'National memory can be 'read' not only by the people of the nation but also by the international public' (2005, p. 346). This observation is particularly relevant at seminal war sites such as those associated with D-Day, because they transcend the interests of individual nations, even those nations directly involved. It is also an important consideration for contemporary multicultural and cosmopolitan societies and the way events of WW2 are memorialised and commemorated. Referring to a recent upsurge in popularity among UK audiences for the DVD reissue of the 1960s film *The Dam Busters*, Paul Gilroy warns that the place of simplistic WW2 triumphalism in contemporary multi-ethnic societies is highly problematic (2004). Demarcations and allegiances between friends and enemies, not particularly clear in wartime can be even more problematic in many contemporary societies that have a complex mix of citizens from different ethnic backgrounds. For example, the choice of designer, design and siting of the Vietnam Veterans' Memorial in Washington DC brought 'regional, ethnic, social and gender tensions ... to the surface' (Johnson 2002, p. 296).

So, D-Day is also the Germans' story. But even this isn't straightforward. Manning the Atlantic wall were thousands of soldiers from the Soviet Union and Eastern Europe. The reasons for belonging to these battalions varied from those who had been conscripted or otherwise forced to join, to those who believed in the Nazi cause, from those trying to escape appalling conditions and death in German POW camps to those who hated the Germans' enemy. The significant presence of Russians and Eastern Europeans, for example, provides a segue into a broader and more complex contextualising of D-Day, such as the conflict on the Eastern Front which absorbed about three quarters of the German army. But how are these stories scripted both in the battle site memoryscape and in the historical discourses and popular culture?

On D-Day some of the Allies also encountered soldiers of the *Indische Legion*, or Free India Legion. Recruited from Indian POWs and Indian student volunteers living in Germany, this force was inspired by Subhash Chandra Bose to help Germany defeat the British and liberate India from imperialism (Munoz 2002). Set to be tried as traitors after the end of the war, they were subsequently released and treated by many as heroes of India's independence struggle. Their legacy continues on with the next generation. For example, while Brigadier Peter Young, who led 6th Commando on D-Day, doesn't hesitate in labelling the soldiers of the *Indische Legion*, 'renegades' (1981, p. 57), the seminal, contemporary, cosmopolitan cultural theorist Arjun Appadurai, whose father was an associate of Subhash Chandra Bose, has had to negotiate with the resulting complexity and what he termed 'a very odd, deep nationalism' (2009 p. 41).

WW2 has been drawn into the general contemporary re-examination of issues around race, gender, ethnicity and colonialism. For example, in the USA there has been a retelling of WW2 from the perspective of Afro-American servicemen. James McBride's book, *Miracle at St Anna* (and the associated film directed by Spike Lee), gives a ficto-documentary account about a few of the 15 000 coloured men of the 92nd Division (Buffalo Soldiers) during the 1944 Italian campaign in the Northern Tuscan mountains (2008). Many felt the war had nothing to do with them, that nothing would change back home in the USA: 'That's what this whole war is. A scam', says one soldier angrily. 'Whites killing whites' (2008, p. 167). One black soldier prefers being in the army, as a Buffalo soldier, even in wartime just so long as he can stay in Italy, which seems to lack the deeply entrenched racism of the USA, especially in the South, and particularly in the US armed forces.

There was strong resistance to giving Afro-American soldiers guns, combat training and combat experience. Strict segregation was the rule. Racial fights between GIs were not uncommon and there were even killings. Tensions ran high, especially in places like Britain during the build-up to D-Day where there was no segregation and black GIs would go to the same cinemas, restaurants and dance halls as white GIs, would flirt with white women and form mixed race relationships. After the war, as the account of Hector, one of the key protagonists in McBride's book, suggests, the racism continued:

> Hector had spent most of his life after the war coming home from work, flopping on the couch, drinking beer, and watching years of television movies that lionized white GIs, who became part of WW2 American lore and myth, so much so that in his daily drunken stupors Hector began to believe that perhaps what had happened to him during the Second World War had not happened at all ... that perhaps he'd dreamed it all. (2008, p. 296)

In terms of the power of media in the racial representations of WW2 and the erasure of non-white American military personnel, Spike Lee criticises Clint Eastwood for not including any black GIs in his film *Letters from Iwo Jima*, claiming that many had fought there (Fox News.com 2008).

Post-WW2 changes in national boundaries and identities also create paradox and complexity. The monument to the Malay Regiment, for example, is located in Singapore which at the time of the fighting was separate from Malaya, although both were part of the British Empire. Briefly part of a united Malaysia after WW2, now the island is an independent nation, dominated by citizens of a Chinese ethnic background. Malaysia, the mainland just to the north, is dominated by people with a Malay ethnic background. The split between the two countries in 1965 was not amicable and a thinly veiled distrust hangs over the narrow strip of water that separates them. Presumably, most of the regiment came from the mainland. Many Malays, as contrasted with those of Chinese ethnicity, opposed British imperialism and supported the Japanese and were comparatively well treated. As a national monument, Muzaini and Yeoh ask which national history is it celebrating (2005)?

While referring to the D-Day landing beaches, Gough insists that we must 'remain acutely aware of the gap between what is there, and what is not there (or there no longer)' (Van Den Abbeele, cited in Gough 2004, p. 249). He continues: 'It is the contemporary visitor's duty to resist the "ease" of imaginary projection' (2004, p. 249). The problem is that the D-Day story is presented, at the memorial sites in Normandy and in the various virtual sites, as being largely unproblematic. The narrative of battle seems straightforward and uncontested—it was for the liberation of a democratic France leading onto a Europe occupied and controlled by the armed forces of one of the most brutal and fanatical dictatorial regimes in history. On the surface at least, it did not appear to be a complex colonial situation as was the fighting in Egypt and other parts of North Africa, Burma, India, Malaya and Singapore, even New Guinea. But, as has been suggested, colonial and racial issues were by no means absent from D-Day. There seemed to be no major atrocities on either side, certainly nothing on the scale of Auschwitz or Dresden. The grand narrative is not completely sanitised however. So, in *Saving Private Ryan* we do see Americans shooting German prisoners. In an official cartoon book version of D-Day, readily available at the Normandy sites, some attempts are made to convey complex ethical moments. Allies are shown shooting German prisoners, plus there are examples of German bravery and honourableness alongside cruelty (Saint-Michel 1994).

The anniversary celebrations of D-Day often bring issues to the surface (Samuel 1994, p. 23). Most recently, the sixty-fifth anniversary was no less controversial. There were disputes about why Queen Elizabeth II, the supreme commander of Britain's armed forces, had apparently not been invited, while the USA's President Obama seemed to be given pride of place. Many attributed it as a snub by the French government, eager to diminish the role of the British in liberating France and to rewrite D-Day as a Franco-American affair. Old strategic disagreements and personality clashes, ones that had existed through D-Day itself, between the British and the Americans also began to surface. Some pointed to the vastly superior media capacity of the Americans compared with the British. Not only was it asserted that the Americans were better at the myth-making of war, but that during D-Day and the battles which immediately followed 'there were about 10 American photographers to every British one ... Most of the footage features American soldiers' (Caddick-Adams, cited in Lawless 2009, p. 80). Even the Russians objected, with some justification, that its considerable part in defeating Germany in WW2 was not recognised at the D-Day ceremonies. Such controversies had circulate around *Saving Private Ryan*—that it distorted historical accuracy by showing American boats landing the soldiers rather than Royal Navy ones which had actually done the job and also by completely ignoring all contributions by countries other than the USA (BBC News 1999).

I'm not saying that the accepted meta-narrative needs to be demolished or rejected. The issue goes beyond pointing to the one-sidedness, omissions and idealisations of the dominant narratives. I'm suggesting that complexity and paradox, an inherent contradictoriness, is too often smoothed out and even effaced. While understandable in the immediate postwar context, such complexity is essential to the contemporary retelling of D-Day and to the re-experiencing by a young generation who have always known a cosmopolitan and multicultural society and identity. It isn't simply a matter of using 'new media' and interactive techniques to attract young people to the old dominant narratives. Important sub-texts need to be given due place, as do entry points into a more complex and contradictory overall narrative. This entails the continual modification, even reinvention of memoryscapes that facilitate 'a process of reflection and debate, however uncomfortable or radical' (Gough 2004, p. 236).

On the one hand the question could be asked about how a contemporary young English person, say, of Indian background might view the landings in Normandy, or how an Afro-American might view them. On the other hand, how might a young 'white' English or American youth say from a mixture of European backgrounds, with an identity that has at least in part emerged from a cosmopolitan, multicultural society, one in which issues of racism and imperialism are at least on the agenda, view the hegemonic D-Day narratives? What about issues around the construction of gender? The worlds from which many of these young people emerge are vastly different to anything that has gone before and certainly to the *Weltanschauung* that constructed the dominant memoryscape.

My children, for example, have grown up in a multicultural milieu with strong German and Italian, and a host of other, heritages. Many friends and relatives come from German and Italian backgrounds. Having seen films such as *Das Boot* and *Valkyrie* they are familiar with the good German soldier of WW2. Films such as *Letters from Iwo Jima* try to portray the Japanese story, the good Japanese soldier. This is the world of popular culture accessible to many young people today. These films form a major part of the virtual WW2 memoryscapes within which they have grown up. The far more immediate controversies of the two Gulf Wars, let alone Vietnam, plus the ongoing conflicts in Iraq and Afghanistan, along with their representation in film and other media entertainment, lie between them and WW2, refracting young people's ideas of the latter.

Spielberg has acknowledged that generational acknowledgement was a central motivation for him making the film *Saving Private Ryan*. In this film, the D-Day events are bookended by a family's contemporary visit to the memorialised landscape. It is an act of remembrance, homage and thanks at an American war cemetery. It is a family, multi-generational visit. Central is the grandfather who experienced it. He is accompanied by his wife, plus their adult children and grandchildren. They are shown in the American cemetery—respectful, silent, and solemn. Such an attitude rightfully has its place in a war cemetery, but no alternative modalities of commemoration are presented. The scene is deliberately personal, generational and national. But this interpretation is unproblematically nationalistic and patriotic, with the Stars and Stripes filling the screen. Past and present forms an unproblematic coupling, as if there have been no significant changes both globally and in the USA itself since 1945. There are, however, numerous examples where contemporary national realignments have precipitated a deep questioning of previously constructed WW2 memoryscapes. Mary Nolan, for example, discusses the changing politics of memory in postwar Germany. Very different interpretations were placed on the Nazi past in West and East Germany resulting in greatly divergent commemorative memoryscapes (2004). The contemporary German reunion has thrown these two very different interpretative paradigms together, in a complex and sometimes fraught process of re-negotiation around issues of 'heroes, victims and perpetrators' (Azaryahu 2003, p. 1). Even what would appear to be a straightforward site—Buchenwald—became the focus of considerable controversy due to its history 'as a Nazi concentration camp, as a Soviet detention camp and as an East German memorial shrine' (2003, p. 1). Anna Krylova details the intense contestation during the early 1990s, after the collapse of the Soviet Union, of 'the war regalia of the Soviet period ... which were no longer unproblematic symbols of the Soviet victory over Nazi Germany' (2003, p. 85).

Conclusion: connecting the past and present

Charles Withers suggests that memory, 'and its expression in memorial or act of commemoration, is a potent means to connect

Figure 2 German gun emplacement, Normandy, June 2008 (author's photo)

historical meaning and contemporary cultural identity' (1996, p. 328). Unusual commemorative features in Normandy are life-size black and white photographs taken during the fighting, which have then been located at the exact sites where they were originally taken. (see Figure 2) Such photographic juxtapositions of battle damaged landscapes with contemporary scenes are not uncommon. But it is a device that is usually confined to books or postcards (for example, Davis 2008). This photographic 'then and now' type of technique seems particularly prevalent in books about D-Day (for example, Woods 1994). However, when the photos are greatly enlarged and located in-situ, a tableau of deceptive simplicity is created, one which dramatically functions as a powerful technology of connection between past and present.

There has been an enormous effort in contemporary museology to devise technologies that bring the past to life, that somehow connect past and present (Vergo 1989; Samuel 1994; Wright 1985). The in-situ photographs are a reminder that the construction of the

D-Day memoryscape is not only concerned with an interpretation of the past but also with an interpretation of the present. While these tableaux greatly simplify both dimensions, at least the past is shown as an event, one whose meaning resonates within the surrounding proliferation of memorialised interpretations, whereas the present is shown as static and unproblematic.

These photo-driven tableaux emphasise that there are two sets of 'truths' that demand narratives of complexity: the historical record of the battle and the present from within which we view, memorialise, and commemorate. As already discussed, from their very inception such memoryscapes, with their attendant interpretations, are often sites of contention and controversy, albeit generally within a limited frame of reference. Some would argue that any memoryscape is inevitably biased and limited by its very nature. What I am arguing is that battlefield memoryscapes have a significant place in the present. They are powerful in terms of education, historical knowledge, ethics, empathy, respect and responsibility. In many cases, such as the D-Day one, attempts are made to deliberately mobilise technologies designed to directly and strongly connect past and present. In the process, a certain representation of the past is connected with a specific representation of the present. The issue here is two-fold. On the one hand these battlefield memoryscapes have overwhelmingly been conceived, designed and staffed by older generations, ones who have had different experiences to the younger generation of today, who have grown up in very different worlds to that which exists now. They prioritised various stories and perspectives in the commemorative narratives. On the other hand, these war memoryscapes seem inadequate in terms of reflecting the complex life worlds of contemporary young people, aspiring to be global citizens. In the not-so-distant future these people will be the custodians of such places.

In cultures where 'minorities' have more voice and are more assertive and respected than before, subplots and other entry points that might once have seemed irrelevant or superfluous now assume a new significance and importance. Also, new problematic framings are being mobilised for battlefield sites, for example around commercial consumerism and various forms of promotion. Crucial signposts that were once assumed to be universally well-known, which mapped out some essential contours of WW2, have either changed meaning or have been forgotten.

Controversies over the accuracy of the narratives, plus their degree of 'completeness' and the appropriateness of the commemorative signifiers, are not only important for historical reasons. Like humour, these debates can introduce uncertainty into the dominant narratives. They loosen, fracture and fragment an otherwise totalising claim to truth. They hence open up possible spaces for different perspectives. In this discussion I have been concerned with the provision of multiple access points into a narrative of sufficient complexity to do justice to the cosmopolitan and multicultural world most of us now inhabit, as well as being appropriate for the new generation that has grown up in this cosmopolitan world.

References

Appadurai, A 'The shifting ground from which we speak', in *Globalizing the Research Imagination*, eds J. Kenway & J Fahey, Routledge, London, pp. 41–52.

Azaryahu, M 2003, 'RePlacing Memory: the reorientation of Buchenwald', *cultural geographies*, vol. 10, pp.1–20.

BBC News 1999, 'Veterans riled by Ryan', March 19, viewed 24 September 2009, <http://news.bbc.co.uk/2/hi/entertainment/299784.stm> .

Beevor, A 2009, *D-Day: the Battle for Normandy*, Penguin, Harmondsworth.

Bougaardt, R 2004, *D-Day: Normandy Revisited*, Chaucher Press, London.

Clout, H 2009, 'From Utah Beach toward reconstruction: revival in the Manche *departement* of Lower Normandy after June 1944', *Journal of Historical Geography*, vol. 35, pp. 154–177.

Davies, W 2008, *In the Footsteps of Private Lynch*, Random House, New York.

Fowles, J 1996, *Advertising and Popular Culture*, Sage, London.

Fox News.com 2008, 'Spike Lee blasts Clint Eastwood for excluding Black GIs from WWII films', May 21, viewed 24 September 2009, <http://www.foxnews.com/story/0%2C2933%2C356822%2C00.html>.

Gilroy, P 2004, *After Empire: Melancholia or convivial culture?*, Routledge, London.

Gough, P 2004, 'Sites in the imagination: the Beaumont Hamel Newfoundland Memorial on the Somme', *cultural geographies*, vol. 11, pp. 235–258.

Hamilton, P 2009, 'Remembering Changi: Public memory and popular media', *Media International Australia*, vol. 131, pp. 136–146.

Heffernan, M 1995, 'Forever England: the Western Front and the politics of remembrance in Britain', *Ecumene*, vol. 2, no. 3, pp. 293–324.

Hutchison, G 2006, *Pilgrimage: A Traveller's Guide to Australia's Battlefields*, Black, Melbourne.

Johnson, N 2002, 'Mapping monuments: the shaping of public space and cultural identities', *visual communication*, vol. 1, pp. 293–298.

Krylova, A 2004, 'Dancing on the Graves of the Dead: Building a Post WWII Memorial in Post-Soviet Russia', in *Memory & the Impact of Political Transformation in Public Space*, eds D Walkowitz and L Knauer, Duke University Press, Durham, pp. 83–102.

Lawless, J 2009, 'Who won war spat rehashed as French snub Her Majesty', *Advertiser*, Adelaide, June 6, p. 80.

Lowenthal, D 1985, *The Past is a Foreign Country*, Cambridge University Press, Cambridge.

McBride, J 2008, *Miracle at St. Anna*, Riverhead Books, New York.

Mitchell, H 2007, 'No laughing matters: The use of humor in texts', *Information Design Journal*, vol. 15, no. 1, pp. 17–20.

Munoz, A 2002, *The East Came West: Muslim, Hindu & Buddhist Volunteers in the German Armed Forces, 1941–1945*, Axis Europa Book, New York.

Muzaini, H & Yeoh, B 2005, 'War landscapes as "battlefields" of collective memories: reading the *Reflections at Bukit Changdu*, Singapore', *cultural geographies*, vol. 12, pp. 345–365.

Nolan, M 2004, 'The Politics of Memory in the Bonn and Berlin Republics', in *Memory & the Impact of Political Transformation in Public Space*, eds D Walkowitz & L Knauer, Duke University Press, Durham, pp. 105–126.

Ray, J 1998, *The Night Blitz, 1940-1941*, Arms & Armour Press, London.

Saint-Michel, S 1994, *D-Day: Operation Overlord, June 6th, 1944*, Memoire d'Europe, Paris.

Samuel, R 1994, *Theatres of Memory*, Verso, London.

Vergo, P (ed.) 1989, *The New Museology*, Reaktion, London.

Young, P 1981, *D-Day*, Bison Books, London.

Withers, C 1996, 'Place, memory, monument: memoralizing the past in contemporary Highland Scotland', *Ecumene*, vol. 3, no.3, pp. 325–344.

Woods, B 1994, *Footsteps of D-Day*, Kent Publishing, Adelaide.

Wright, P 1985, *On living in an old country*, Verso, London.

Filmography

Saving Private Ryan 1998 dir Steven Spielberg

Charlotte Gray 2001 dir Gillian Armstrong

Miracle at St. Anna 2008 dir Spike Lee

Letters from Iwo Jima 2006 dir Clint Eastwood

Blackadder Goes Forth 1989 (BBC)

Life is Beautiful 1997 dir Roberto Benigni

Life is a Miracle 2004 dir Emir Kusturica

*M*A*S*H* 1970 dir Robert Altman

Dad's Army 1968-1977 (BBC)

Das Boot 1981 dir Wolfgang Peterson

Valkyrie 2008 dir Bryan Singer

The Longest Day 1962 dir Ken Annakin, Andrew Marton, Bernhard Wicki, Gerd Oswaild, Darryl F. Zanuck

Gameography

The Band of Brothers

Brothers in Arms

Medal of Honour

Call of Duty

Chapter 2

Follies, Furphies and Fugitives: Dan Billany and the Italian prisoner of war camps at Rezzanello and Fontanellato

Paul Skrebels

University of South Australia

Background

In 1949 a book appeared which, given the strange story of how it managed to see the light of day, let alone the difficult circumstances under which it was written, had the odds stacked firmly against its being published at all. Yet published it was, albeit under a title and in a form unintended by its authors, who were no longer around to have a final say in either. The book was *The Cage*, and that first edition produced by Longmans, Green and Co contained frontispiece portraits of its authors, Dan Billany and David Dowie, with the notation 'whose fates are unknown'. In addition, inside the dust-jacket was a request that 'Anyone who has information which may lead to the discovery of the fate' of its authors 'is asked to communicate with the publishers.'

Billany and Dowie were English prisoners-of-war in Italy during the Second World War when they embarked on documenting their experiences in a work they called *For You the War is Over*. Dan Billany had established himself as a published author with a very successful detective novel, *The Opera House Murders*, before joining the British Army and his subsequent capture in North Africa in mid 1942. He would have another book, *The Magic Door*, for children, published during his time of incarceration. He also had written the manuscript of another work, a partly autobiographical, partly fictionalised account of his war service and first weeks of captivity, which would be published as *The Trap* in 1950. His co-author, David Dowie, had

Figure 1 Title page of the manuscript of For You the War is Over *(Billany family estate)*

no record of prior literary achievement, yet three prison camps and—making use of whatever scraps of paper they could get hold of—several drafts later, *For You the War is Over* was nearing completion when events overtook it.

By September 1943 the Italian war effort—at least in its broadly Mussolini-led phase—had collapsed, and Billany and Dowie, along with thousands of other Allied prisoners, walked free from their POW camps.[1] A full reconstruction of those days, as they attempted to avoid recapture by the Germans while finishing the final draft, can be found in Reeves and Showan's biography, *Dan Billany: Hull's Lost Hero* (1999). Suffice it to say that before Billany and Dowie disappeared into the countryside, never to re-emerge, the manuscripts of what would turn out to be *The Cage* and *The Trap*, as well as notebooks containing earlier drafts, notes and illustrations, were left with Italian farmer Dino Meletti, who in 1946 posted them to Billany's father, Harry, in England.

In the 1990s all of this material, together with other related matter, was donated by Billany's family to the Imperial War Museum, London. The manuscripts reveal that while the work eventually known as *The Trap* was published in accordance with Billany's final draft, the one that became *The Cage* had undergone considerable editorial intervention. This involved leaving out the many illustrations originally accompanying the story, plus many other excisions and alterations to the text, so that although, as Reeves and Showan describe, the eventual appearance of *The Cage* in May 1949 generated a run of very favourable reviews, it was only a partial representation of the work intended by its authors.

I have been undertaking a project to restore the work to its original state, which has involved two stages. The first has been to revise the text of the 1949 edition so that it more accurately reflects that of the final draft manuscript, and to reintegrate the illustrations, hitherto unavailable to the public except for a tiny sample in Reeves and Showan's book. The next stage entails the addition of notes and appendices drawn from material in the Billany-Dowie notebooks, from letters sent to the family by Billany, and from broader background and contextual information, as aids to contemporary readers and researchers.

There is no question that *The Cage*, even in its first published form, is a remarkable work and a noteworthy addition to the canon of World War 2 and prisoner-of-war literature. It is hoped that in its restored form as *For You the War is Over*, it will be recognised both as a unique and ground-breaking tour-de-force in war writing, and for its potential to contribute even further to our understanding and appreciation of the times and the people involved.

During the course of my research into Billany and Dowie's lives as POWs, in 2008 I visited the sites of the second and third of their three Italian prison camps: PG (for *Prigione di Guerra*, literally 'War prison') 17 at Rezzanello, near Piacenza, and PG 49 at Fontanellato, near Parma. What follows is an account of their experiences at these places, related largely in their own words, and interspersed with my own observations and reactions to each.[2] Along the way, support will be elicited from some of the more pertinent studies of POW life in the WW2 generally and Italy specifically, as well as from the writings of Billany and Dowie's fellow POWs. These turned out to be a particularly 'literary' group, some of whom, more fortunate than the subjects of this study, managed to assemble an impressive body of published work of their own after the war.

PG 66 Capua

By way of a prelude to that, however, something needs to be said about the first camp they arrived at in Italy, PG 66 at Capua, near Naples. Although I wasn't able to visit this site, PG 66 represented a key stage in the formation of the particular, if not necessarily unique, POW culture inhabited by Billany and Dowie, as well as offering a backdrop against which the rather different 'worlds' of Rezzanello and Fontanellato might more clearly be delineated. This difference is in turn significant to *For You the War is Over*, in that its authors took advantage of the changed circumstances of the move from PG 66 to implement a 'turn' in both the narrative and the style of the work.

Billany and Dowie, although from different units, were captured by the Germans within days of each other in early June 1942 at the disastrous Gazala battles in North Africa. Later that month they arrived at PG 66, a typical 'barrack-hut-and-barbed-wire camp ...—the model for the camp in the film *The Great Escape*' (Gilbert 2006, p. 69), and the sort in which fellow POW, crime-writer-to-be Michael Gilbert saw fit to set his own novel of betrayal and mass escape, *Death in Captivity* (first published 1952).[3] It was also the only one of the three camps they were sent to that contained predominantly 'other ranks'—that is, privates and NCOs—as prisoners. However, Billany, Dowie and the other officers were housed in a separate compound within the larger camp, 'the little world (seventy yards square) in which we were to spend the next six months' (Billany & Dowie 1949, p. 5).[4] It consisted of

> four huts, six latrines, and a wash-house. Fifty of us slept in each of three huts; the fourth was the dining-hut, where also we wrote letters, played bridge, held lectures, and so on. If we wanted exercise, we walked round the huts. (Billany & Dowie 1949, p. 11)

In one of the sixty-one numbered letters and postcards written while a POW to his immediate family—his father Harry, mother Elsie and sister Joan[5]—Billany paints a homely word-picture of the prisoners' daily routine:

> At a quarter to eight in the morning George is getting out the breakfast things, Alec is folding his blankets, John is brushing his hair, and I am in bed. There is a shout, "Coffee," and everybody grabs a mug and dashes off to the coffee-dixie, from which an officer serves morning coffee. If it seems cold, I remain in bed. At eight o'clock an English-speaking Italian N.C.O. comes in and shouts "roll-call". We assemble in three ranks: an Italian captain calls the roll. Then we cook our breakfast. Nowadays we have made another cooker, a portable tin one known as the "Hellbrew", and for the sake of getting all the food piping hot we often cook on both our old stove & the Hellbrew simultaneously, porridge & tea on one, ham roll &

Figure 2 *Billany's sketch of POWs setting up the 'Hellbrew' at PG 66 (Billany family estate)*

> tomatoes, bacon, bully or what have you on the other. Then we eat: this is the best part of the morning. We finish breakfast usually soon after nine … After this I wash and shave, read the newspaper, and do a spot of writing, if time. Or I read a canto or two of the "Faerie Queen". Then lunch is served, at about 12 o'clock: macaroni or rice soup, meat or fish, vegetables. In the afternoon there may be a lecture ("Tibet", "Advertising", "Tiger-shooting" "Rare Books" etc.) or a walk. We prepare tea at 3:30, usually a big meal, apple-pudding, creamed rice, pilchards, cheese, bread & jam, etc. Then I write some more, till dinner at 6: and after that we have tea, cocoa or hot milk, and I settle to a quiet, studious evening. What a life! (Billany, letter no. 22, 13 November 1942)

While Billany's biographers are quick to point out that letters such as this were 'written to reassure the family', in that it 'vastly exaggerates the amount and quality of the food' (Reeves and Showan 1999, p. 117), it nevertheless sets the general tone for the ways the POWs coped with their new situation. It also demonstrates the degree to which social groupings were formed early on—initially as 'syndicates' for pooling precious resources and sharing chores—but which usually survived the two further shifts of venue, where syndicates were no longer essential for day-to-day survival. Certainly the 'Capua' section is the book's most 'matey', being made up largely of short episodes focusing on the interactions between all residents of the compound: their use of latrines, the cook-house and other shared facilities; their participation in lectures, the library, and other attempts to pass the long hours of captivity; their maintaining a common 'front' in the face of their Italian captors; and, a leit-motif running throughout the Capua section, their reliance on the 'rumour-bell' that draws all the POWs into a single community as it keeps them informed of the latest news and gossip:

> *Bong!*
> —Quiet!
> —New rumour that we're moving.
> —Where?
> —Don't know. Somewhere north.
> —When?
> —Next week some time.
> —Rot. We're going into the new compound next month.
>
> (Billany & Dowie 1949, p. 75)

PG 17 Rezzanello

Rezzanello lies about 20 kilometres south-west of Piacenza in the Emilia-Romagna region, in the hills overlooking the lower Trebbia valley. It's not a town or village in the usual European sense, so much as a collection of dwellings and commercial buildings strung out along the road leading up from Gazzola, the municipal centre, to neighbouring Monticello. The dominant feature, apart from the church of San Savino, is the *castello* (= castle) of Rezzanello, and it was to this, in its wartime guise as PG 17, that Billany, Dowie and some 150 other officers were relocated by the beginning of December 1942:

> we are uprooted, and are now in a permanent camp for officers. The camp is actually a castle, surrounded by the most beautiful country you could ever imagine—wooded mountain country, just like Derbyshire or Cumberland or Wales. After our last camp, it is damned cold, but we shall survive that without difficulty: and we are very much more comfortable, and very cheerful and glad of the change. There's a splendid library here, too, with dozens of really first-class books that I've always wanted to read.
> (Billany, letter no. 25, 1 December 1942)

When, sometime around May 1943 and already settled into their third camp, PG 49 at Fontanellato, Billany and Dowie embarked on writing *For You the War is Over*,[6] its authors would use the move to PG 17 to shift their narrative perspective from the 'outer' life of the community—representing 'the period of physical adjustment to prison' (Billany & Dowie 1949, p. 87)—to the 'inner' lives of individual POWs. They hoped to show, by dealing 'principally with emotional and psychological reassessments', how this time of 'tension and turmoil' might lead in turn to 'a catharsis, a new resolving of emotional factors, a new synthesis, so that the prisoner goes out a new man into a new world' (1949, p. 87). Their method is to concentrate the story largely on the relationship between Dowie and the fictional character of Alan Matsen—an apparent projection of Billany's homosexuality—and the eventual reconciliation between Matsen's infatuation with Dowie and the latter's initial rejection of him.[7] They achieve this by switching the narrative to a series of entries drawn from Dowie's diary, interspersed with rather intense, 'drawing-room-scene' dialogues between Dowie, Matsen, and Billany himself (who, intriguingly, remains a separate character).[8]

Figure 3 *Billany's impression of the castello (Billany family estate)*

Figure 4 *The castello in 2008 (author's photo)*

Dowie's diary entry for the same day as Billany's first letter from Rezzanello reveals some of the reasons underpinning the book's change of focus:

> 1st. [December] Arrived at Rezzanello after a typically Italian journey. It is an amazing place—we expected to find hundreds of prisoners already here, in the usual barrack-huts, but this is a castle—very fake castle—with turrets and narrow stairs—a Folly?—and we have it to ourselves. There are "Other Ranks" here, batmen, who have been prisoners so long that they no longer consider themselves in the army. Afraid they will be jolted shortly. There is exercise—Volley Ball—and a good library. But it's bloody cold! (Billany & Dowie 1949, p. 87)

Wandering through the *castello* today, it's easy to see its potential as a retreat from the real world, in addition to—yet also distinct from—a prison's usual function of separating its inmates from the outside. Although a genuinely ancient edifice, its frequent alteration since it was founded in 1001 makes it seem the more recent 'folly' the POWs believed it to be. This air of fantasy heightens the sense of the *castello* as an 'other place', a utopia or—paradoxically, given its role as a prison camp—as an escape from the outside world. This last is by no means as outlandish a proposition as it might sound. After all, in fiction for centuries, Italy generally and castles specifically have served as settings conducive to love, intrigue and other romantic goings-on—especially for Northern European readers and audiences already predisposed to regard both Italy and castles as exotic. In the real world, sequestration from the distractions of everyday life has long been offered by 'fortified' monasteries and convents—Monte Cassino being a particularly apt example here—and latterly, by exclusive schools, health institutes and other such establishments, customarily occupying castles and stately homes. Billany and Dowie themselves recognised the *castello* as such, particularly in contrast to their subsequent move to PG 49 Fontanellato with its larger POW population and a return to a more humdrum prison-camp existence.

In fact, the notion that POW life, particularly in the more exclusive officers' camps, was an escape from the real world was generally acknowledged even at the time. According to one study, 'The everyday responsibilities and worries [POWs] faced as servicemen and, above all, as civilians had largely been removed from them', with one inmate observing that 'they had the luxury of not having to think for themselves what to do, of being, however badly, fed, housed and clothed.' Tellingly, this POW concludes, 'In a way it was a return to childhood' (Gilbert 2006, p. 97). How much more removed from the adult world the officer prisoners must have felt at Rezzanello, whose dormitory rooms and cloisters would have reminded many of their school days; there was even a supply of other ranks to do the 'fagging'. Indeed,

> Many commentators observed how similar the camps were to public schools and how easily the POWs seemed to fit into their new environment, with the more privileged groups usually in the ascendant. (Gilbert 2006, p. 96)

While neither Billany nor Dowie were products of the English public school system, their time in the army no doubt inculcated a certain degree of the 'officer and gentleman' ethos, if only to accustom them to the services of the military version of the public school 'fag', the officer's batman.[9]

Even so, there were a few things to get used to first of all, principally the lack of heating in the dark old stone building. The climate at PG 66 Capua was such that the lightweight khaki drill clothing worn by most of those captured in North Africa was adequate. Not so Rezzanello, where pullovers and items of the British Army's serge battledress were in much demand and short supply. Billany complained that it was 'too cold to sit down to much reading, or any writing except letters'. His solution was to 'spend a good deal of time walking briskly about the garden, or digging—we have a patch which we want to turn over to weather, so that we can put in some vegetables in February'

(Letter no. 26, 8 December 1942). More formal walks were organised for the POWs, which also introduced them to the local scenery in its various forms, as Dowie's diary entry for 5 December indicates:

> Went for first walk today—fifty of us marching in threes, sentries on either side. There's a church and a couple of shops outside, just on the corner. Two girls leaning out of window above one of the shops. Very satisfying to the eye, but not much use to the inner man. (Billany & Dowie 1949, p. 92)

Not only the church but also the shops—although certainly somewhat altered since then—still stand on the corner across the road from the grounds of the *castello*. The sight of the girls notwithstanding, the principal appetite nurtured by all this exercise was hunger: 'Could have eaten a horse when I got back. Had to be content with our daily bread' (1949, p. 92).

However, once, presumably, proper advantage was being taken of the batmen's services, and the system of pooling Red Cross parcels—which also involved putting a certain proportion aside for Christmas—was in full swing, life at Rezzanello took on a rosier hue, at least according to Billany's letters home:

> Since last writing, Christmas has happened: we all had a very good time, more food than we could eat ... We went down periodically to eat, and then returned to our rooms, like gorged snakes, to digest what we had swallowed.

Such was the spirit of camaraderie and celebration that he was able to add:

> On Christmas Day itself we had a very comic sing-song and show. Altogether I'm bound to say that, for a Christmas in prison, it was Bloody Good, and, as Tom Ockleston, our Senior British Officer, said after dinner, it was a time we shall be glad to remember. (Letter no. 29, 29 December 1942)

Figure 5 *Billany's sketch of 'View from ante-room window, Rezzanello, Dec. 30th, '42' (Billany family estate)*

Soon, even the climate was an aspect of life at the *castello* to be appreciated:

> We've had a good deal of snow in the last four days, and the countryside is very lovely, fir and pine trees piled with snow, etc. I've made a sketch of one of our views, which will give you some idea, when I get back. (Letter no. 30, 5 January 1943)

Despite the chummy goings-on at Christmas, Rezzanello, like all good places of retreat, ultimately gave rise to self-reflection. In an aside to his sister Eva's husband, Charles Wilkin,[10] Billany looks back on his own time as a student studying desperately hard to matriculate from Hull Municipal Technical College (the 'H.M.T.C.' referred to in the letter) in order to get into university:

> To be quite honest, I don't now envy you your H.M.T.C. job: God, I shiver when I think of that grim, barrack-like, prison-like place where you're harnessed, where you have to torture both literature and life—Christ, "Macaulay on Pitt"! Honest, I'm not sure, now, that I don't prefer this prison: at least there's no treadmill, and one has the chance, walking in odd corners of the castle, of meeting oneself now and then. (Letter no. 30, 5 January 1943, original emphases)

Unsurprisingly, therefore, Rezzanello proved the perfect place to develop the story of Alan Matsen's infatuation with and pursuit of Dowie. On the one hand the venue made more plausible the outward manifestation of feelings which—with their overtones of the adolescent crush so readily fermented in the cloistered life of the private school—might not find full expression amid the communal bustle of 'hutted' camps such as PG 66.[11] On the other, Billany and Dowie had obviously found the time and space for serious introspection about the nature of their friendship and the clash of sexualities that it represented.

PG 49 Fontanellato

After barely four months at PG 17, Billany and his fellow officer POWs were sent to a new camp, PG 49 at Fontanellato, 'a large, pleasant village in the plain of Lombardy' (Billany & Dowie 1949, p. 156), approximately twelve kilometres north-west of Parma (and only some 60 km directly east of Rezzanello). With the departure of most of its inmates, PG 17 Rezzanello seems to have been wound down as a POW camp,[12] with its history as such subsequently—and perhaps conveniently, as will be noted later—forgotten. PG 49 Fontanellato was another single-building type of camp, but a rather different one, as Billany informed his family:

Figure 6 *Billany's impression of the* orfanotrofio nazionale
(Billany family estate)

Figure 7 *The orfanotrofio in 2008, in its current guise as the Fontanellato community hospital (author's photo)*

I'm writing from the new camp. It's a big new building, very clean and airy, and with some advantages over the castle, though so far we have less room to exercise: we all arrived a few days ago. (Postcard, unnumbered, 3 April 1943)

His next correspondence went into more detail:

> It is an ex-orphanage, the sort of place which philanthropy usually considers appropriate to defenceless kids: immense staircases and hall, tons of marble, stained glass, and windows too high for children to look out of. All cooking is centralised, so that life is rather like that of an hotel – pleasant enough. Our compound is to be enlarged, so we should soon have plenty of room for exercise. The weather is fine, cool, windy: drier than an English April. All the trees are budding: the green plain and the distant Alps are pleasing if not so lovely as P.G.17. (Billany, Letter no. 43, 10 April 1943)

The building, now located well within the boundaries of Fontanellato, but during WW2 sitting just on its edge, was indeed intended as the region's *Orfanotrofio Nazionale*. However, when Italy threw in its lot with Germany in 1940, the government requisitioned it before completion and turned it into PG 49 for officer prisoners. Depending on the source consulted, PG 49 held '540 mainly British officers' (Gilbert 2006, p. 73), or 'Some 600 prisoners-of-war, mainly junior officers' (Absalom 1991, p. 127), or 'six hundred and fifty prisoners, much overcrowded' (Billany & Dowie 1949, p. 136). Although 'lacking in space for recreation', according to 'an inspector from the Swiss Legation in Rome' it was one of the better camps in Italy, with adequate rations of food, tobacco and alcohol, including 'a glass of wine and of vermouth each day' per man (Gilbert 2006, p. 73). Not in dispute is the surprising number of published works on life as a POW and beyond that emerged after the war by former inmates of the *orfanotrofio*. Besides Billany and Dowie's uniquely contemporary account, these include Eric Newby's *Love and War in the Apennines* (1971), perhaps the best known work and by PG 49's most 'canonical' author; Stuart Hood's darkly brooding *Pebbles from My Skull* (1963); Michael Gilbert's fictionally set but authentically reconstructed *Death in Captivity* (1952); Tony Davies' memoir of escape and evasion, *When the Moon Rises* (1974); and the more recent *Assisted Passage* (1994) by Ian English.[13]

Given the obvious degree of willingness by its inmates to articulate their thoughts and experiences of life in PG 49, it is unsurprising perhaps that Billany and Dowie shifted the narrative perspective of *For You the War is Over* even further towards the inner lives of its characters. The section 'Fontanellato' thus consists entirely of a series of internal monologues revealing their hopes and fears for the present and the future. Chronologically and historically these culminate in the downfall of Mussolini, the pending surrender of Fascist Italy, and the implications this has for the release (or otherwise) of the POWs. Emotionally and psychologically they reveal a reconciliation of sorts between Alan and David, and their awareness that at this personal level, too, 'For us the war was over' (Billany & Dowie 1949, p. 190).

Unfortunately for both Billany and Dowie and all the other prisoners, the war was by no means over; ironically, what actually followed was more the stuff of the adventure novel or the ripping-yarn than their own deeply self-reflective history of the camps had developed into. PG 49 was run by Colonel Eugenio Vicedomini, 'a First World War veteran who had fought with the British in 1917-18' and regarded by the POWs 'as a gentleman of the old school' (Gilbert 2006, p. 73). He and his sixty or so staff and guards 'got on reasonably well with the British officers' (2006, p. 73), so-much-so in fact that as the anticipated Italian Armistice approached, he and the Senior British Officer, Lt Col Hugo De Burgh, had negotiated the formal release of the whole camp. Thus on 9 September 1943, the day after the Armistice was signed, 'the departure of prisoners of war was achieved in a completely organized and disciplined fashion' (Absalom 1991, p. 127). This was done with the full cooperation of their Italian captors:

> when ... the warning was given, Italian officers cut down a section of the wire and within 10 minutes De Burgh was able to lead the whole camp population ... out into freedom, marching in formation ... When the Germans arrived shortly afterwards they found the midday meal and wine prepared, but not a single Allied prisoner ... (1991, p. 128)

PG 49 apparently was the only camp where this kind of arrangement had been made; in some, prisoners were held by their Italian captors until the Germans turned up to convey them to camps in Germany; in others, the notorious 'Stand fast' order issued by Allied Headquarters was complied with by their SBOs, even when the Italian commandants threw open the gates and gave prisoners carte blanche to escape. The Allied order was a misguided attempt to prevent the Italian countryside from being flooded with aimless and vulnerable ex-prisoners. In reality it created a great deal of resentment between ordinary POWs and those on their own side who tried to uphold it, sometimes to the extent of placing armed guards along the wire.[14] At the same time there was no way that camps could have been liberated by Allied troops, whose lines were too far away, and besides, the Germans were proving too swift and efficient in filling the void made by the collapse of the Fascist regime. Those who swooped on PG 49, finding it empty, took out their frustration on Vicedomini who,

> gallant to the end, had remained alone to confront them: he was arrested and sent to a camp in Poland from which he returned at the end of the war, broken in health, to die soon afterwards. (Absalom 1991, p. 128)[15]

The POWs, initially at least, were more fortunate, because while the Germans were scouring the *orfanotrofio*,

> the mass of escapers from PG49 were hiding in the bushes in a dried-up river bed and in nearby vineyards little more than two miles away and the inhabitants of Fontanellato ... were arriving in large numbers to bring food, civilian clothes and offers of help, or simply to satisfy their curiosity. (1991, p. 128)

Despite the charity shown to the POWs, their escape ordeal was just beginning. Some chose to head north to the Swiss border; many more headed south towards the Allied lines. And, as Absalom and others have shown in their accounts of this strange period, while many released POWs continued to receive outstanding support from the Italian people, the vast majority were swept up by the ever-vigilant German and still loyal Italian forces and finished the war in other camps. The rest, if they didn't eventually find their way back to the Allies, were killed outright trying to escape, or died fighting with partisans or from exposure in the mountains during the harsh winter of 1943-44, while still others, Billany and Dowie among them, disappeared without trace.[16] The *orfanotrofio*'s war wasn't over yet, either. Following its demise as PG 49, the building was plundered by the German army, then set up as an officer-cadet school under Mussolini's revitalised Italian Socialist Republic. As a result, it was bombed by the Allies and so not opened as an orphanage until after the war, in 1948. It remained as such until 1982, when it underwent a further transformation into its current role, as a community hospital ('Beata Vergine del Santo Rosario' 2001).

Follies or Furphies?

It has already been pointed out that the occupants of both PG 17 and PG 49 had developed a number of 'furphies'—to use the Australian soldiers' term meaning 'a rumour' or 'a false story' (*Macquarie Dictionary* 1990)—regarding each site's origins and, in the case of Fontanellato, its prognosis. In each case these proved to be mistaken and yet, like all legends, they contain elements of truth and insight.

The POWs believed that the *castello* of Rezzanello, with its 'turret like a Christmas cake standing up at each corner', was a relatively recent folly:

> The batmen had a story that it was built a hundred and fifty years ago by a Scotsman who married an Italian heiress, and certainly there was something dimly Scottish about it. It was like "Lucia di Lammermoor"—as Scottish, and as Italian. It was perhaps the scene-painter's impression of the stage-manager's impression of Donizetti's impression of Walter Scott's impression of the late seventeenth century; and the arch which led into the garden was

faced with white marble as if the local funeral furnisher had been called in to finish the job. (Billany & Dowie 1949, p. 90)

Billany and Dowie's witty embellishment of the batmen's story turns the *castello* into a set of Chinese boxes, none of which is any more authentic than the other. Certainly the visitor today is confronted with a kind of architectural palimpsest, a site coated in layers of history each of which has effectively obliterated the preceding layer. The sign put up by the current owners (in Italian and English) is meant to convey a sense of those layers:

> The castle was built in the 10th century. In 1001 the bishop Sigifredo of Piacenza gave the castle to the S. Savino Benedictine Order. In 1212 it was occupied by the Piacenza Guelphs. When they left it was taken over by the Milanese Ghibellines. It came into the hands of the Chiapponi family in the 15th century and in 1796 ownership passed to the Scotti family. Thanks to Marquis Ferdinando Scotti, the castle became a luxurious manor. In the 19th century the new owner, the surveyor Giuseppe Manfredi, authorized architect Camillo Guidotti to restore it. The castle was then owned by the Genoese Lombards, the Counts of Cigala Fulgosi and by the Orsoline nuns. It was eventually purchased by the current owners. The interior was decorated with "stylish" ornamental motifs by Francesco Jelmoni and Arnoldo Ghittoni. The castle is surrounded by 70.000 square metres of grounds. With its trapezoidal mass collection of planta it is one of the biggest and best kept Castrensi castle [*sic*] in the county of Piacenza.

Clearly missing in this potted history is any mention of the war, nor is there a memorial in the building or the grounds marking the conflict.[17] In taking the tour of the castello (at five euros a visitor), I tried, in Italian, to draw the owner on the topic of its role as PG 17. The best I could get out if him—before his attention was diverted by a young couple obviously impressed enough by its faux gothic ambience to book the castello for their wedding—was that, yes, it had served as an SS command post at some stage, and yes, he believed that some British officers had been interrogated there. This may point to some aspect of Rezzanello's use after the Armistice, but it has nothing to do with PG 17.

The *orfanotrofio* at Fontanellato also came in for the POWs disdain, this time as part of anything emanating from Mussolini's dictatorship:

> It is a new building, Fascist in inspiration, and very large. One of the peculiar necessities of a nation afflicted with Fascism seems to be liberal accommodation for orphans ... The building is pretentious. It looks solid, but is actually flimsy, and will not last very long. The whole structure is subordinated to a vast pompous façade in what might be called the Municipal-Flamboyant manner.
> (Billany & Dowie 1949, p. 136)

Eric Newby (1972, p. 31) thought it

> so unstable that if anyone jumped up and down on one of the upper floors, or even got out of bed heavily, it appeared to wobble like a jelly. To those of us who were lodged on one of these upper floors, it seemed so unstable that if any bombs fell in the immediate neighbourhood it would collapse.[18]

However, unlike present-day Rezzanello, at Fontanellato there has been a concerted attempt to remember the war years and what they represent for the community. A plaque placed prominently in front of the grounds of the former orfanotrofio, now the *Ospedale di Fontanellato,* tells a very different story from the sign at Rezzanello:

> This memorial recalls in this 40th anniversary the English and Allied prisoners of war whom, interned in Concentration Camp PG 49, the people of Fontanellato, following the Armistice of 8 September

> 1943, aided and sheltered at the risk of serious reprisals. Fontanellato 11 September 1983.[19]

Paradoxically, therefore, although Billany and Dowie and their mates were wrong about, or refused to credit, Rezzanello's actual long history, ultimately they were right in one respect. Today the castello is a venue for conferences and weddings, where newlyweds can imagine themselves part of a romanticised and sanitised history of the kind evoked in the works of Sir Walter Scott. Here the past is elided with the present and any inconvenient details, such as Italy's role in the Second World War, are simply erased and forgotten. Not so Fontanellato which, as the plaque in front of the ospedale suggests, is part of a well-established tradition of commemoration. The town's name is celebrated in the annual 'Fontanellato luncheons' held by the Monte San Martino Trust, which was set up in 1989 by former POW J. Keith Kilby and other veterans (representing many camps) as a mark of their gratitude to ordinary Italians for helping them after the 1943 Armistice.[20] Moreover, since the war Fontanellato itself has seen a number of reunions between ex-prisoners and townsfolk and their families (Roger Absalom, conversation 14 May 2008). More significantly, however, the POWs' original scathing assessments of the orfanotrofio were misplaced. Sixty-five years later the supposedly shoddy and short-lived building is a thriving community hospital whose past life as PG 49 is not only readily acknowledged, but which stands as a symbol of and a tribute to the common humanity of former enemies.

Acknowledgements

I wish to thank the following for their assistance in writing this article:

- Roger Absalom of Sheffield Hallam University for sharing his expertise with me concerning POWs in Italy generally and at Fontanellato specifically;
- Jodi Weston-Brake, executor of the Billany family estate, for

allowing me virtually unlimited access to the family archive, and for her hospitality to my wife and me during our visit, her support for my project, and her unbounded enthusiasm to see her Uncle Dan gain the public recognition we both believe he deserves.

NOTES

1. With Mussolini's forced resignation as dictator on 25 July 1943 following pressure by the armed forces and the Fascist Grand Council on King Vittorio Emmanuele III, a caretaker government under Marshal Badoglio took over. When the Allies began landing on the Italian mainland in September, Badoglio secretly negotiated an armistice to end Italian resistance, which came into effect on 8 September. See Collier (1971, chapters 7 and 8) for a detailed account of these events.
2. Richard Holmes's, 'new way of doing biography, which he calls footstepping' (Slattery 2008), is particularly apt in the case of my 'vanished' subjects, Dan Billany and David Dowie: 'Holmes said biography becomes "a kind of pursuit, a tracking of the physical trail of someone's path through the past, a following of footsteps. You would never catch them ... but maybe, if you were lucky, you might write about the pursuit of that fleeting figure in such a way as to bring it alive in the present"' ('Renowned Biographer' 2008).
3. It was turned into the film *The Danger Within* (1958), starring the usual line-up of stalwarts including Richard Todd, Michael Wilding and Richard Attenborough. The plot of Gilbert's novel obviously suited a camp with separate huts rather than the single orphanage building of PG 49, where he actually ended up with Billany and Dowie.
4. For ease of reference, *The Cage* (1949 edn) has been quoted from in preference to the MS version, *For You the War is Over*.
5. To his other sister, Eva, who was already married and living apart from the family, Billany usually wrote separately.
6. Billany's letter no. 50, dated 30 May 1943, mentions, 'I've struck out on something new, a book in collaboration with David Dowie, and I really think it's going to be a corker'.
7. Dowie wasn't gay, but his rejection of Alan's affections in the book is based neither on sexual repulsion nor bigotry against homosexuals. Rather, he finds Alan's attempts to ingratiate himself pathetic and desperate, and is put off by the latter's general air of maudlin self-pity.
8. 'Dan', freed from his attraction for Dowie by the creation of 'Alan', is thus able to represent the detached and rational side of Billany's

character. Billany obviously had considerable trouble coming to terms with his sexuality in real life, but wasn't afraid of exploring it to impressive effect artistically.

9. Billany and Dowie were both from a mix of working class and lower middle-class backgrounds. Billany was an avowed Socialist and Dowie had served in the ranks before being commissioned.
10. Wilkin was to die tragically suddenly in 1946 following a gall-bladder operation, leaving Eva a widow with two small children (Reeves and Showan 1999, pp. 156-7).
11. See also Newby 1972, p. 42 for his view of PG 49 Fontanellato as 'more like a public school than any other prison camp I was ever in', and his assessment of 'English preparatory and public school life' as 'hell'.
12. At least according to Roger Absalom (conversation 14 May 2008).
13. The dates in parentheses are the original publication dates; all have been reprinted, Hood's work in 1985 under a new title, *Carlino*. Major Ian English was one of only 24 British officers to be awarded the Military Cross three times during the Second World War. His third award was for action on Mont Pinçon in the NW Europe campaign in August 1944; he had rejoined his former unit, the 8th Bn Durham Light Infantry, following his successful return to the Allied lines in December 1943. Maj English died aged 86 in April 2006 ('Major Ian English' 2006).
14. The wording of the 'Stand fast' order was as follows: 'In the event of an Allied invasion of Italy, Officers Commanding prison camps will ensure that prisoners-of-war remain within camp. Authority is granted to all Officers Commanding to take necessary disciplinary action to prevent individual prisoners-of-war attempting to rejoin their own units' (Absalom 1991, p. 27). It had been issued some months before the Allied landings, possibly by General Montgomery, the commander of the British forces set to invade Italy, himself. Apparently neither Churchill nor the War Cabinet in London were aware of the order, Churchill being in favour of the rescue of the POWs 'at any cost' (1991, p. 27).
15. Some sense of what Vicedomini must have experienced in the camp in Poland can be gleaned from another splendid and very imaginative POW account, this time from the Italian perspective, Giovanino Guareschi's *My Secret Diary* (1958). Guareschi, author of the Don Camillo stories among others, was one of thousands of Italian Army officers interned after the Armistice by the Germans for refusing to serve in the forces of the new fascist puppet state, the Italian Socialist Republic.
16. See Reeves and Showan (1999, pp. 142–166) for a summary and discussion of Billany and Dowie's time after their release from PG 49, and of the efforts made to discover their whereabouts after the war. Roger Absalom's research among the files of the Allied Screening Commission,

held in Washington DC, led to his finding chits signed by Billany, Dowie and fellow escapee Alec Harding to compensate families in villages as far south as Tornimparte and Capistrello near l'Aquila in the Abruzzi Mountains; the last is dated 20 November 1943. Absalom is convinced that they perished around that area, just short of the Allied lines (Reeves and Showan 1999, p. 166; Absalom, conversation 14 May 2008).

17. This is in contrast to the *castello* of Monticello located about two kilometres of winding road further up from Rezzanello. There the visitor will find not only a memorial to those who fell in the First World War, but quite an elaborate one to local partisans in the Second.
18. The *orfanotrofio* exacted its revenge on Newby, who shortly before the Armistice slipped on the marble staircase while wearing hobnailed boots and broke his ankle. Both he and author Michael Gilbert were the sole occupants of the camp hospital at the time—Gilbert with a boil on his backside (Newby 1972, pp. 29, 45 and 48). Newby's account of life in PG 49 offers some very interesting contrasts and correctives to Billany and Dowie's.
19. My translation, with acknowledgement to my colleague, Dr Giancarlo Chiro. The original inscription reads: '*Questa lapide ricorda nel quarantesimo anniversario i prigionieri di guerra inglesi e alleati qui internati nel campo di concentramento P.G. 49 la popolazione di Fontanellato che dopo l'armistizio del 8 settembre 1943 li aiutò e li nascose a rischio di gravi rappresaglie—Fontanellato 11 settembre 1983*'.
20. The Trust provides about 20 bursaries annually for young Italians to study English at schools in England for a month, and 'supports walks along Freedom Trails in Italy to commemorate the escapes by POWs and the hospitality given to them during their attempts to reach safety' (*The Monte San Martino Trust*).

References

Primary sources

Billany, D, letters and other correspondence to the family while in captivity, Billany family archive.

Billany, D and Dowie, D, *For You the War is Over*, MS and notes held in the Imperial War Museum, London, file 96/14/1.

Secondary sources

Absalom, R 1991, *Strange Alliance: Aspects of Escape and Survival in Italy 1943-45*, Olschki, Firenze.

‘Beata Vergine del Santo Rosario, Fontanellato (Parma)’ 2001, *Maria di Nazareth*, viewed 30 March 2009, <http://www.mariadinazareth.it/Immagini%20Miracolose/beata%20vergine%20del%20S.R.%20di%20Fontanellato.htm>.

Billany, D & Dowie, D 1949, *The Cage*, Longmans, Green and Co, London.

Collier, R 1971, *Duce: The Rise and Fall of Benito Mussolini*, Collins, London.

Davies, T 1974, *When the Moon Rises*, Futura, London.

English, I 1994, *Assisted Passage: Walking to Freedom in Italy 1943*, privately published; reprinted 2004, Naval and Military Press, Uckfield, East Sussex.

Gilbert, A 2006, *POW: Allied Prisoners in Europe*, John Murray, London.

Gilbert, M 1952, *Death in Captivity*, Hodder and Stoughton, London.

Guareschi, G 1958, *My Secret Diary*, Gollancz, London.

Hood, S 1963, *Pebbles from My Skull*, Hutchinson, London.

The Macquarie Dictionary 1990, Macquarie University, NSW.

‘Major Ian English’ 2006, *The Telegraph* (Obituaries, 29 April), viewed 15 April 2009, <http://www.telegraph.co.uk/news/obituaries/1516919/Major-Ian-English.html>.

The Monte San Martino Trust, n.d., viewed 15 April 2009, <http://msmtrust.org.uk/home/>.

Newby, E 1972 (orig. pub. 1971), *Love and War in the Apennines*, Readers Union, Newton Abbott.

Reeves, V A & Showan, V 1999, *Dan Billany: Hull’s Lost Hero*, Kingston Press, Kingston upon Hull.

‘Renowned Biographer Richard Holmes gives Seymour Lecture in Canberra’ 2008, *Canberra Times*, 15 September, viewed 17 April 2009, < http://www.canberratimes.com.au/blogs/colin-steele/richard-holmes-in-canberra-and-shameless-publicity-stunts/1272557.aspx?storypage=5>.

Slattery, L 2008, ‘In the footsteps of past masters’, *The Australian*, 10 September, viewed 17 April 2009, <http://www.theaustralian.news.com.au/story/0,25197,24320202-12332,00.html>.

Chapter 3

Putting away childish things: the realities of conflict

Nigel Starck
University of South Australia

Paul of Tarsus understood the complex shifts, in mood and sentiment, which colour the journey from childhood to maturity. His letter to the school at Corinth has been enshrined in the New Testament as a persuasive reflection on the process:

> When I was a child, I spake as a child, I understood as a child, I thought as a child; but when I became a man, I put away childish things. (I Corinthians 13:11)

The apostle's text resonates euphoniously in attitudes to military conflict, notably among those of us who were precocious readers during the immediate postwar years. In youth, we were intoxicated by a potent literary genre; as adults, we are confronted by evidence that is variously affirming and discomfiting. The suppositions of childhood are, consequently, either given credence or put comprehensively away.

My own journey along this path was aroused at its outset by books of escapist character. That terminology has a literal application, for as an obsessive young reader of the 1950s I devoured prisoner of war escape stories of extraordinary valour and inventiveness. Their titles seduced me: *Escape or Die* (Brickhill 1952), *Boldness Be My Friend* (Pape 1953), *They Have Their Exits* (Neave 1953). The narrative invariably lived up to expectations too, as RAF navigator Richard Pape demonstrates (p. 230) in recounting his Gestapo interrogation:

> I was alive ... I was dead ... I was ascending ... I was descending. I burned with a volcanic heat. I froze with cold. I was floating with delicious and bewildering ease ... I was plunging through roaring water ... And then, as it all receded, I saw the stone wall, and I was pressed against it, erect and trembling.

Pape acknowledges an inspirational meeting with Wing Commander Douglas 'Tin Legs' Bader, whose own story of escape—along with some considerable triumph over physical adversity—was told by the art's most prolific recorder, Paul Brickhill. His *Reach for the Sky* (1954, p. 278) contains a particularly graphic passage in describing a violent parachute descent from a crippled Spitfire, when one of Bader's artificial legs became trapped in the cockpit:

> Then the nightmare took his exposed body and beat him and screamed and roared in his ears as the broken fighter dragging him by the leg plunged down and spun and battered him and the wind clawed at his flesh and the cringing sightless eyeballs. It went on and on into confusion, on and on, timeless, witless and helpless ... till the steel and leather snapped.

The language alone, not just the heroics, supplies a vivid—if necessarily vicarious—engagement with conflict. In Bader's story, there is an inevitable progression to the serial escapers' castle, Colditz. All the facets of their calling flowered within its walls: courage, stoicism, intrigue, failure, humour, madness, and occasional success. Major Pat Reid, whose 'home run' was assisted by Bader at its break-out phase, discloses in his book, *The Colditz Story*, the influence of World War 1's literary heritage on both his boyhood and his manhood:

> When I was a boy at school, I read with avidity three of the greatest escape books of the First World War ... [so] when the fortunes of war found me a prisoner in an enemy land, the spirit enshrined in them urged me to follow the example of their authors ... I can think of no

> sport that is the peer of escape, where freedom, life, and loved ones are the prize of victory, and death the possible though by no means inevitable price of failure. (Reid 1952, p. 17)

There was no sport attached to the Jewish persecution memoirs. The most popular of them, *The Diary of Anne Frank* (first published in English 1952; critically revised 1989), did, however, contain an element of sexual dalliance, a topic generally avoided in the prisoner of war exploits:

> Do you think that Mummy and Daddy would approve of my sitting and kissing a boy on a divan – a boy of seventeen-and-a-half and a girl of just under fifteen? I don't really think they would, but I must rely on myself over this ... But there is indeed a big 'but', because will Peter[1] be content to leave it at this? ... [H]e is a boy! (Barnouw and van der Stroom, 1989, p. 609)

The nearest that the old lags of Colditz had ventured in discussing sex was to recall the brazen attempt by a French inmate to escape dressed as a woman. He almost succeeded, being foiled only by the accident of dropping his elegant wristwatch and the chivalrous, but ultimately unfortunate, intervention of a British officer who urged the guards to return it. Such incidents typify the voice that, regardless of actual story or author, can be heard in the Colditz books: the voice of the irrepressible, if nominally grown-up, schoolboy (the captive serviceman) who simply will not capitulate to the dictates of the obdurate schoolmaster (the commandant). It was an effortless affair, accordingly, for me to slip into the realm of metamorphosis; empathy and self-identity with my heroes in print assumed addictive proportions.

It was less easy, though, to imagine being incarcerated in a concentration camp, for there had been nothing in my brief existence to supply a comparative measure. This extract from a Dachau diary (Neuhäusler 1960, p. 49), for example, delivers such a heinous passage of inhumanity that readers of any age would surely have resisted projecting themselves into its pages:

> The worst punishment of all was the 'standing bunker'. In a room about the size of a telephone kiosk ... the prisoner was compelled to stand three days and three nights and was given only bread and water; every fourth night he came into a normal cell, ate prisoners' fare and was allowed to sleep for one night on a plank bed. Then the three days' standing began again.

There was the Cold War too. It generated a variation on the theme. This time the emphasis was on the novel, often of *roman à clef* inclination, fomented by the building of the Berlin Wall. John le Carré's *The Spy Who Came in from the Cold* (1963) led the charge, spawning a remarkable twenty-three impressions in less than four years and enabling its writer to make a personal transition from middle-ranking spook to celebrated author:

> Darkness had fallen, and with it silence. They spoke as if they were afraid of being overheard. Leamas went to the window and waited, in front of him the road and to either side the Wall, a dirty, ugly thing of breeze blocks and strands of barbed wire, lit with cheap yellow light, like the backdrop for a concentration camp. East and west of the Wall lay the unrestored part of Berlin, a half-world of ruin, drawn in two dimensions, crags of war. (pp. 9, 10)

Here, the imagery conveyed to the reader was more of the *film noir* variety: ominous shadows, trench coats under sickly street lights, sleet, deception. It proved similarly fecund, with Len Deighton and Frederick Forsyth joining le Carré in a corpus of clandestine plots.

The Wall now is down, the camps have been cleansed, and the techniques of World War 2 escapology rendered archaic. Forged identity cards and fake passes would be unable to fool sophisticated detection and recognition processes of today. The literary legacy endures nevertheless. It owes its survival to the *lieu de mémoire* (site of memory) factor, a theory formulated by the French historian, and member of *L'Académie française*, Pierre Nora. He has argued (1989) that a significant entity, in this instance a body of writing, has the power to become a symbolic element within memorial heritage. The point is developed by Valerie Krips in her book, *The Presence of the Past: memory, heritage, and childhood in post-war Britain* (2000): prepare

> [B]ooks are more than the narratives they contain: they operate in the world as material objects, things in themselves. The books of childhood are in a special phenomenal relation to the world and the child's experience of it: they are likely to be one of the objects through which the young child comes to interact with the world. (Krips, p. 16)

Captivated, therefore, by the sum of my own bookish phenomena, I have long undertaken pilgrimages to sites of significance. Five of those locations offer direct relevance to the escape stories, to the persecution memoirs, and to the Cold War literature: Colditz Castle; Anne Frank's house in Amsterdam; Dachau concentration camp; the Berlin Wall; and the Stasi Museum in Leipzig. To what degree, though, can they sustain the influential quality presence of the books, extending juvenile imagination into adult gratification?

Colditz is unquestionably the most imposing of the quintet. There has been a castle on this cliff over the River Mulde, an hour-and-twenty minutes by rambling village bus from Leipzig, for a thousand years. The fortress to which Wing Commander Douglas Bader, Captain (as he was then) Pat Reid, and Lieutenant Airey Neave were despatched after their intransigence at other camps was built by Augustus the Strong (Elector of Saxony 1694–1733). They encountered walls more than two metres thick, floodlighting, barred windows, barbed wire, and a garrison that 'outnumbered the prisoners at all times', elevating escape to 'a formidable proposition' (Reid 1952, p. 59).

Today, painted white rather than its former grey and transformed

Figure 1 *Colditz Castle: a prison for serial escapers transformed today into a youth hostel with guided tours, in English, of the former cell blocks. (author's photo)*

into an upmarket youth hostel, it welcomes travellers to a conducted tour in English. The guides are plainly rather proud of the erstwhile guards' inability to prevent eighteen 'home runs' by British, Dutch, and French escapers; it demonstrates a certain tolerance, a willingness by both sides to play the game.[2] They also make the point, forcibly, that Colditz was staffed by the German army, not the degenerates of the SS.[3] Accordingly, there were deliveries of Red Cross parcels and mail, the Geneva Convention's protocol on prisoner of war treatment was largely recognised, and the perpetrators of failed escapes would pose in their disguises—and, judging by the look on their faces, not altogether unwillingly—for the town photographer after their recapture.

Deprival of liberty and survival of bipartisan bonhomie are apparent in the pictorial displays and the unpretentious souvenir shop. Glass cases contain escape memorabilia: papier mâché rifles, lookalike uniforms made from blankets, and handcrafted identity cards. A tunnel dug through forty metres of rock by French officers has been retained as a symbol of determination; there are pictures of the dummy, made by the Dutch, which would be paraded in close formation to fool the head-count while a break-out was in progress.

The guide points to the window where Bader conducted a makeshift orchestra, watching sentries instead of players. The music would stop when, by Bader's reckoning, an escaper could safely elude a sentry's beat. Higher up, in an attic overlooking a terrace on the ramparts, is a model of the Colditz glider. The real craft was readied for its launch from there—to fly over the river and onto a meadow, with a crew of two—by the combination of dropping a concrete weight and releasing a giant elastic band fashioned from the bladders of footballs and basketballs. It never flew, however. A shoot-on-sight policy introduced late in 1944, along with the executions that followed a mass escape in Silesia, brought a new-found mood of caution. The glider would be used, its construction team therefore decided, only if reprisals for bombing raids were directed at the inmates of Colditz. Fifty-five years later, and watched by seven Colditz veterans, a replica completed a circuit of an airfield in Hampshire, proving that their design was aeronautically impeccable.

Despite the threat of being shot, Lieutenant Mike Sinclair of the King's Royal Rifle Corps remained intractable, and the tour concludes with an acknowledgment of his zeal. He made so many escape attempts from a variety of camps that his photograph was posted at police stations throughout the Reich. '*Der Rote Fuchs*' (the Red Fox), as the Germans called him because of his ginger hair, covered a lot of territory before being hunted down: to the Bulgarian border, to the Dutch frontier, and to Cologne. But his ninth bid for freedom, on 25 September 1944, was both desperate and fatal. He hauled himself over a barbed wire fence during an exercise excursion, ignored the shouts of '*Halt, oder ich schieße!*', and was gunned down (Reid 1962, p. 561). Seven months later, Colditz was relieved.

Its state of preservation enables the adult visitor, especially one informed in youth by the literature, to obtain a firm impression

Figure 2 Tunnel vision: a French escape team hacked through forty metres of rock before being detected and sent into the Colditz solitary confinement block for their trouble. (author's photo)

of conditions that prevailed in the war. Reality dovetails with expectations; the old lags have told their stories well.

Anne Frank's House in Amsterdam offers—like Colditz—an experience set in aspic. A 1995 project restored the front of no. 263 Prinsengracht so that it looks just as it did when Otto Frank operated his business ventures there, making jelly ingredients and spices. Behind no. 263 is the annex where the Frank family, as Jews eluding transportation to the gas chambers, went into hiding on 6 July 1942. Once more, reading and reality are in alignment so far as the physical properties of the site are concerned. Anne Frank's diary delivers a precise guide to the interior design:

> To the right of the landing lies our 'Secret Annexe'. No-one would ever guess that there would be so many rooms hidden behind that plain door painted gray. There's a little step in front of the door and then you are inside ... If you go up the next flight of stairs and open the door, you are simply amazed that there could be such a big room in such an old house by the canal. (Barnouw & van der Stroom 1989, p. 214)

But then agitation intrudes upon *lieu de mémoire*. She writes (p. 217) of brightening up the bare walls of her bedroom with her 'picture postcards and film-star collection ... This makes it look much more cheerful'. Clinging yet to the walls after more than sixty years, these images continue to serve as *agents provocateurs* to the senses. It is at once distressing and beguiling, rather than cheering, to see the fifty-two images that comprise her antidote to isolation: postcards of Britain's Princess Elizabeth and Princess Margaret, clippings of Greta Garbo and the Lane Sisters, and photographs of the Dutch royal family in their Canadian exile. The tourists begin queuing well before the 9am opening, and they parade through this hide-out in sustained hush. This has become a sacred place. The natural inclination to silence echoes the daytime imperative that Anne was obliged to observe: 'Not a drop of water, no lavatory, no walking about, everything quiet' (Barnouw & van der Stroom, p. 401).

To heighten the experience and—as much as is possible—to understand the implications of the Frank family's betrayal after their two years in seclusion, one must shift from this sanctuary to the crowded horrors of the concentration camps. Otto and Edith Frank, with their two daughters and their four companions from the no-longer secret annex were taken initially to Auschwitz. Anne and her sister, Margot, were later transferred to Bergen-Belsen, dying there in the typhus epidemic of early 1945.

The first of this network of camps was Dachau, opened in 1933, initially as an internment centre for the National Socialists' political opponents. Communists, Social Democrats, and monarchists—who had passionately disagreed with each other before the Nazi regime—were thrown together in so-called 'protective custody' at this converted munitions factory on the outskirts of Munich. They were soon joined by Jehovah's Witnesses, Jews, gypsies, and those who had been denounced in a remorseless array of Kafka-esque circumstances. Dachau, according to Barbara Distel's official history (1972, p. 1) became 'a powerful reservoir of slave labourers ... [and] for the SS, the ideal training ground for murder'.

Its wrought-iron gates still carry the inscription *Arbeit Macht Frei* ('work makes you free'). That work, as Johannes Neuhäusler has recorded in his memoir *What Was It Like in the Concentration Camp at Dachau?* (1960), included:

- The unnecessary digging and shifting of soil and stones from one location to another, along with the rolling of the camp streets by 'ten to sixteen starved prisoners' harnessed to heavy rollers, driven forward by 'a row of SS-men and Capos carrying leather whips'. (p. 36)
- Plantation work in 'a huge square wrested from the Dachauer marshes at the cost of countless human lives', where men were yoked to ploughs and harrows in the cultivation of tea and vegetables. (p. 37)
- The gravel pit, the worst of all: 'Without rest and without peace ... the sun rises higher ... Here a prisoner stretches himself and utters a groan, there another rests a little on his shovel. Instantly, the butt of a rifle in the ribs or a kick brings them back to their drudgery'. (pp. 37, 38)
- The snow commando. 'The SS would not tolerate snow within the limits of the camp ...The snow commando had to work eight hours daily, always on the go.' Those who collapsed were left lying on the ground, often contracting pneumonia. (p. 38)
- Transport. Heavy four-wheeled wagons, with prisoners in the shafts, shuttled from the station to the workshops, from the gravel pits to the kitchens, and—inevitably—to the burial heaps. Sometimes, the task was deliberately trivial in terms of its payload: 'We must go to the station. And what has to be brought to the station? A parcel of screws, as big as two cigar boxes. In our innocence we ask ourselves why eighteen men plus three sentinels plus a five-ton lorry [are needed] ... We do not know that prisoners and sentinels and lorry may never separate. That is the supreme principle'. (p. 40)

It is noticeable that among contemporary pilgrims to Dachau, strap-hanging on the free bus from the railway station to the camp forecourt, are parties of German schoolchildren. They, in their youth, are permitted to learn—without revisionism—the excesses of their nation's past. So they are shown the crematorium and the gas chamber, the stakes from which manacled inmates were suspended, the whipping block, and evidence of the medical experiments under which prisoners were exposed to malarial mosquitoes, subjected to barbaric variations in pressure and temperature, and deliberately infected with ulcerating disease that led to 'purulent wounds as big as the palm of my hand' (Neuhäusler 1960, p. 64).

Figure 3 The main gate at Dachau, with its declaration Arbeit Macht Frei ('work makes you free'): the evidence of the crematorium, the whipping block, and grotesque medical experimentation serves to counter that assertion. (author's photo)

Dachau offers a graphic engagement with the reality of conflict, to the extent that the travel publisher Lonely Planet has advised (2000, p. 458): 'The experience can be so disturbing that we don't recommend it for children under age 12'. Further north in Germany,

Berlin contains a more complex lesson in achieving the transition from juvenile fancy to mature understanding. For this city, so scarred and divided and eventually united in belligerence, is 'a place haunted with landscapes that simultaneously embody presences and absences, voids and ruins, intentional forgetting and painful remembering' (Till 2005, p. 8). And it has The Wall. This unseemly accretion of concrete and graffiti inspired the spy story of the 1960s, natural successor—in the reading of my adolescence—to that earlier fascination with the prison camp genre:

> Berlin was perfect. A romantic past and a tragic present ... A place of dramatic contrast where an author's wildest flights of fancy not only actually happened but could be *guaranteed* to continue to happen. You could sit down and write a book about the Berlin Wall and bet your bottom dollar that by the time it came out the Wall would still be standing. (Eager 1989, p. 14)

When Charlotte Eager wrote those words for the British magazine *The Spectator*, the Wall had just crumbled. Chunks of it were seized as souvenirs; some 600 000 East German citizens flocked to the shops and bars of West Berlin; each was offered 100 Deutsche Marks as pin money. The contrast was remarkable. In the preceding twenty-eight years of the Wall's existence, seventy-eight people trying to escape through or over it had been killed.

Four sections, along with just one of the 215 watchtowers, survive under protection as historical monuments. That would seem only fair, for the Berlin Wall—in art and in life—assumed 'the most acute expression, materially and symbolically, of the global rift between the politics of cold-war ideologies' (Kamm 1996, p. 61). But in the thaw, and with the tour buses ambling benignly past, it now appears to be of little more substance than the wall presented by the Rude Mechanicals in *A Midsummer Night's Dream*, where Bottom ordered that one of his fellow players should 'have some plaster, or some loam, or some roughcast about him, to signify wall' (Harrison 1957, p. 48).

Figure 4 Checkpoint Charlie reincarnated: no sniffer dogs, no razor wire, and shooting now limited to that of the photographic kind. (author's photo)

Colditz has maintained its imperious presence; Anne Frank's house delivers its eponymous heroine's spirit; Dachau endures as an assault on civilised senses; but the Wall, as a literary emblem and as a force in youthful imagining, is spent. The 4000 sniffer dogs have been muzzled; the 5000 vapour lamps vaporised. Checkpoint Charlie, a dangerously crepuscular setting in the books, has become today only a flashpoint for digital cameras; at one euro a time, a 'sentry' poses with tourists. He is in US military uniform, but his tie is loose at the collar, he wears a goatee, his shoes are unpolished. There is an absence of verisimilitude.

This de-scaling of the reader's outlook is advanced apace in Leipzig, where in 1989 demonstrations in favour of the Wende (the 'turning point' in recent German events) were at their most animated. Much of the reason for that citizen unrest can be found within a building known as the Runde Ecke (the 'round corner'), formerly the headquarters of East Germany's Ministry for State Security (the Stasi). The grubbiness of cold war pursuit is revealed in its interrogation cells and in the trappings of surveillance: wigs and moustaches, crude microphones in office desks, a grotesque padded 'stomach' concealing a camera, devices for the undetectable opening of mail. And, of singular unpleasantness, there is a collection of jars with vestigial smell samples taken from suspected dissidents. The Stasi would obtain a swab during an interview, store the odour, and then—with the aid of dogs trained for the task—track their subsequent activities.

All this is on show, free to citizens and visitors, in the building's new incarnation as a repository of espionage. It is at once engrossing and repellent, and devoid of any scent of the adventure or romance emitted by the books. Here, at the Runde Ecke in Leipzig, it is manifestly time to put away some of one's childish things.

Notes

1. Peter van Pels, who—with his parents—shared the Frank family's hide-out.
2. The figure of eighteen is authenticated by the military journal *After the Battle* (no. 63, 1973). It refers to the number of successful escapes from within the bounds of Colditz itself. Others, taking the estimated total to as many as thirty-one altogether, were achieved by Colditz prisoners from outside locations (notably hospitals).
3. The SS (*Schutzstaffel*: 'protective squadron'), originally Adolf Hitler's personal bodyguard, grew to a complement of 800 000. Its most notorious section was deployed in the concentration camps.

References

Barnouw, D & van der Stroom, G (eds) 1989, *The Diary of Anne Frank: the critical edition*, Viking, London.

Brickhill, P 1952, *Escape or Die*, Evans Bros, London.

Brickhill, P 1954, *Reach for the Sky*, Collins, London.

Corinthians I 1953, *The Holy Bible*, Oxford at the University Press, London.

Distel, B 1972, *Dachau Concentration Camp*, Comité International de Dachau.

Eager, C 1989, 'Wall Games', *Spectator*, 2 Dec, p. 14.

Harrison, GB (ed.) 1957, *William Shakespeare: A Midsummer Night's Dream*, Penguin, Harmondsworth.

Kamm, J 1996, 'The Berlin Wall and Cold-War Espionage: visions of a divided Germany in the novels of Len Deighton', in *The Berlin Wall: representations and perspectives*, eds E Schürer, M Keune, & P Jenkins, Peter Lang, New York, pp. 61–73.

Keune, M 1996, 'Preface', in *The Berlin Wall: representations and perspectives*, eds E Schürer, M Keune, & P Jenkins, Peter Lang, New York, p. v.

Krips, V 2000, *The Presence of the Past: memory, heritage, and childhood in post-war Britain*, Garland Publishing, New York.

le Carré, J 1963, *The Spy Who Came in from the Cold*, Victor Gollancz, London.

Lonely Planet: Germany 2000, Lonely Planet Publications, Hawthorn.

Neave, A 1953, *They Have Their Exits*, Hodder & Stoughton, London.

Neuhäusler, J 1960, *What Was It Like in the Concentration Camp at Dachau?*, Roch-Druck, Höchstädt an der Donau.

Nora, P 1989, 'Between memory and history: les lieux de mémoire', *Representations* 26 (Spring), pp. 7–25.

Pape, R 1953, *Boldness Be My Friend*, Elek, London.

Reid, P 1952, *The Colditz Story*, Hodder & Stoughton, London.

Reid, P 1962, *Colditz*, Hodder & Stoughton, London.

Till, K 2005, *The Berlin Wall*, University of Minnesota Press, Minneapolis.

Chapter 4

'We're not German': How Austria marks the Nazi years

Sue Page
University of South Australia

Cultures of forgetting, as well as cultures of remembrance, are part of Maria Tumarkin's study of traumascapes—those sites of great loss and tragedy, caused by the violence of nature or humanity. She argues that such places

> are never empty or blank. Even when they are covered in ruins, even when they look like they could be on the moon, even when they have shopping centres built on top of them, these sites are filled with meaning and history. All places in our lives are palimpsests, containing many different layers of the past on top of each other. (Tumarkin 2005, p. 225)

It was, in part, what I was exploring in Austria in 2008, and specifically, the layers of the Nazi era past, and how they are—or are not—acknowledged not only in Mauthausen, the single concentration camp that has been preserved out of the main camp and forty-nine permanent sub-camps which were on Austrian territory (Marsalek 1996, p. 7), but in the very streets, towns and cities where the trauma was instigated.

One of the first issues is whether the past—particularly a traumatic one—should be marked or remembered at all. In many countries, such as Australia, it is not only seen as a good thing, but a critical one. There does not have to be a personal connection in order for people to have strong feelings; think of the debate about how the Port Arthur killings should be marked. It does not even have to be on Australian soil for us to claim ownership of what we see as sites of national tragedy—Bali, Gallipoli and the Kokoda Track are all recent examples where despite the fact that they are foreign places, Australian public and political opinion on the memorialisation of events, and protection of the places where these events took place, has run high. There appears to be a common belief that these places belong to us by virtue of the trauma suffered there by Australians. Diplomatically and politically, we assert moral rights; we expect to have an influence in what happens there; we expect that not only will these sites serve as memorials in some form, but that they will be given ongoing maintenance and protection. We are possessive of our traumascapes, wherever they may be. Memorials provide us with a physical focus for an emotional and psychological connection to the past and to those directly affected by it. But this attitude is not universal.

It is primarily a cultural question, but will not be answered the same way by all within a specific culture. In Germany, for example, it was the postwar generation that made national self-examination, acknowledgement of responsibility, owning up to the truth and investigation of the past so important. Their parents and grandparents—those who participated in and observed the atrocities of the Nazi era—did not welcome this revisiting of and answering for the past. Yet the children succeeded. With few exceptions, their Austrian peers took a different stance.

> Cultures of forgetting have appeared from ancient to modern times, and, for countries such as Spain with its Civil War, Russia with its Stalinist past, or Austria with its national socialist crimes, it is difficult to argue that forgetting and repression do not work. These countries have integrated the atrocities committed during a generation or more into their respective collective biographies and have achieved a peaceful transition to the next generation. (Schlink 2009, pp. 47–8)

Yet not all Austrians take that view. For example, the Gusen Memorial Committee is an Austrian-registered non-government organisation, whose webpage[1] is sponsored by the Austrian Broadcasting Corporation. It is dedicated to informing people, particularly Austrian teenagers[2], about the history of Mauthausen's sub-camps, which in the late 1990s were marked by memorials. Writing in 1998, the then-President of the International Mauthausen Committee, Jos. Hammelmann, said:

> The prominence of memorials in the three villages affected show the former victims of persecution how Austria, despite pressure from the extreme right, opposes tendencies to play down or even deny Nazi crimes. (Gusen website)

Such memorialisation is rare; the culture of forgetting appears to be an apt description of most Austrians' perspective on the twentieth century past. I do have misgivings about Schlink's term 'integrated'. To integrate anything, which is a conscious and deliberate act, means first to acknowledge its existence. Yet, evidence this has happened in Austria is scanty. While tourists can find information on the Internet about museums dedicated to Jewish history, there appears to be nothing about the many other victims in the 1930s and 40s. Even when the past is acknowledged, it is partial and reluctant; in sharp contrast to Germany, Austria's Nazi era history is corralled away from daily view.

> In Berlin, the city's past and present share the civic space with each other. The past is not merely relegated to museums and historic sites; it is the present's equal, debated, venerated and continuously in the public eye (Tumarkin 2005, p. 121).

Other aspects of history are far more palatable to Austrians. Ball gowns are prettier than uniforms. Palaces are more attractive than camps. Music is more appealing than gunshots. I understand that, completely. Which country would not want to present its best face to the tourists, or reflect that aspect to its own citizens? But not all of Austria's past was civilised. Nor were all Austrians perpetrators;

Austrian politicians, artists, journalists, pacifists, trade unionists, gays, socialists, as well as Jews, were the first victims following the Anschluss. However, as shown later, the enthusiasm with which Austrians flocked to the Nazi cause shocked even veteran commentators.

One of the most striking aspects of the public discourse regarding the National Socialist past is the positioning, which ignores Austrian responsibility for actions taken there by Austrians, in favour of their self-representation as a subjugated nation forced to follow orders from Berlin.

That is what gave this essay its title. While staying in Salzburg for a conference I met a young man who worked in the hotel. He was in his early twenties, the age of many of my students, good at English, and funny. In the process of several conversations, he talked about his work ambitions and planned travels. He came from a small village in the mountains, moving to Salzburg to work. He was friendly, intelligent and had an interest in what was happening in the world.

I asked him for suggestions on what I should see once the conference was over. Where, for example, should I go around the Salzburg area for information or sites related to the Second World War? I'd already arranged to go to Linz and Mauthausen later in the trip, but had not found anything in Salzburg that commemorated what had happened there in the 1930s and 40s. Not even in the Rathaus area, which had been the hub of Salzburg's Jewish community pre-war. Tourism was Mozart-oriented; the closest thing to information about the Anschluss or what occurred afterwards was the popular *The Sound of Music* tour (complete with sing-a-longs). 'Mauthausen's the place to visit,' he said. 'There's nothing around here.' He'd been to Mauthausen once on a school trip, but didn't remember much about it. I asked what he'd been taught about the Second World War at school; he said they'd 'done' it, but mostly it was about Germany and not Austria. 'Aren't you curious,' I asked? 'About your family and what they did? About neighbours, and friends' families?'

'It's different here,' he said. 'We're not German.' One of his friend's grandfathers had been in the SS, he knew, but he had never asked him about it. Nor, as far as he knew, had his friend. But as to everyone else, he didn't know. 'Not even your family?' 'No. We don't talk about that kind of thing.' Possibly by chance, that was the last time we talked. I went to Vienna.

Vienna was once the home of the largest German-speaking Jewish population in Europe. Of the 200 000 Jews who lived in Austria in 1938, 180 000 lived in Vienna (Morse 1968, p. 199). This amounted to 'more than 10 percent of the city's inhabitants' (United States Holocaust Memorial Museum website).

The actions of Viennese during and after the Anschluss horrified journalists who had been covering events in Germany for years. Take William Shirer:

> What one now saw in Vienna was almost unbelievable. The Viennese, usually so soft and sentimental, were behaving worse than the Germans, especially toward the Jews. Every time you went out you saw gangs of Jewish men and women, with jeering storm troopers standing over them and taunting crowds shouting insults, on their hands and knees, scrubbing Schuschnigg slogans off the sidewalks and curbs. I had never seen quite such humiliating scenes in Berlin or Nuremberg. Or such Nazi sadism. The S.A. and S.S. were picking hundreds of Jews off the streets or hauling them out of their homes to clean the latrines in the barracks and other buildings seized by them. Foreign Jews or foreigners whom the Nazi thugs fancied looked like Jews were also seized and put to work at menial tasks. (1984, p. 314)

Morse quotes reports from the *New York Times* in the days after the Anschluss:

March 16 [1938]

Adolf Hitler has left behind him in Austria an anti-Semitism that is blossoming far more rapidly than ever it did in Germany. This afternoon the Jewish quarter of Leopoldstadt was invaded by triumphant crowds that called families from their houses and forced them to kneel and try to scrub from the pavements slogans such as 'Hail Schuschnigg' which were part of the former Chancellor's plebiscite campaign. This humiliation was carried out under the supervision of Storm Troopers wearing swastika armlets. The crowds were composed ... of some of the worst elements of the population, assembled to jeer at the Jews ... (in Morse 1968, p. 200)

Reporter Ed Murrow had been in Vienna before Shirer arrived. He had watched the beatings and lootings and arrests and humiliations, and according to Shirer,

From a window of my apartment, Ed [Murrow] and I, after a stiff drink, watched the S.S. men emerge from the Rothschild house and piling their booty in waiting trucks. I was anxious to see what the city, now that Hitler had taken it over, looked like. So we crept down the stairs, waited until our guards were away from the entryway, and sneaked out on tiptoe in the darkness. The streets were fairly quiet. Ed said all the Jews had pretty well been rounded up and arrested – several thousand of them – as well as several more thousand Socialists and followers of Schuschnigg. The former chancellor himself, Ed said, was under Gestapo arrest but no one knew exactly where.

We tramped around the inner city for an hour and then adjourned to a bar off the Karntnerstrasse. By this time, Ed had settled into a lugubrious mood – one I would get to know well. He was depressed by what he had lived through in Vienna all week; the hysteria of the crowds, the shouting and boasting of Hitler, the sadism of the Nazi bullyboys in the streets. A few evenings before in this very bar, he said, he had seen a Jewish-looking man get drunk and slash his

> throat with an old-fashioned straight razor he had pulled from his pocket. (1984, p. 313)

Baron Louis Rothschild, referred to above, managed to buy his way out of the country by signing over ownership of his steel mills to the Hermann Goering Works. Many other Austrian Jews also managed to get out by handing over their wealth and possessions—thanks, largely to one man. SS Captain Adolf Eichmann was not a well-known Nazi to start with, but he instituted a Central Office for Jewish Emigration in Vienna. This later became the mechanism by which Jews were exterminated.

> By May 17, 1939, nearly half of Austria's entire Jewish population had emigrated, leaving only approximately 121,000 Jews in Austria (all but 8,000 in Vienna). Though the pace of emigration slowed to a trickle with the increasing threat of war and its outbreak in September 1939, another 28,000 Jews were able to leave Austria between May 1939 and the middle of 1942. (United States Holocaust Memorial Museum website)

By 1944, the Museum's figures show that only about 6000 Jews remained in Austria. Most of those were married to non-Jews; the rest were in hiding. It is unclear how many chose to stay in Austria after the war. But it should not have surprised me that there was so little of the longstanding Jewish heritage to be seen in Vienna, outside museums. Young Austrian Harald Edinger, a former intern at the United States Holocaust Memorial Museum, said in a podcast on 1 January 2009:

> And in today's Austria, you hardly ever encounter a blatant form of antisemitism. But one simple reason might be that nowadays, there is [*sic*] hardly any Jewish people living in Austria. So this loss of Jewish heritage in Austria is quite sad, actually, given the country's—and especially Vienna's—long and rich Jewish history. So as I said, antisemitism in its original sense, it may be hard to find

Figure 1 *Memorial to the Austrian victims of the* Shoah *(author's photo)*

Figure 2 Shoah *monument at Judenplatz (author's photo)*

> here in Austria. What is more present, however, is sort of ignorance or a resentment towards more and more Holocaust education, commemoration. Because from some people, you hear that they think the guilt of this country, the debt of this country is already paid off.

Ignorance and resentment may be a recent phenomenon, but given the comments by my Salzburg acquaintance, it appears unlikely. Lawrence Langer makes the point that people tend to have one of two reactions to Holocaust memorialisation:

> Imagining that shadow, reimagining it, living uneasily beneath it and its implications, understanding those implications (for the past and the future) – our natural instincts are to avoid the whole enterprise, or to generate rays of sunlight that will radiate through its darkness. (Langer 1982, p. 29)

My impression is that Austrians prefer the former. There is some commemoration, at least of the Jewish victims. The memorial to the Austrian victims of the *Shoah*[3] is off a square near the Museum Judenplatz—an annex to the Jewish Museum Vienna.

I was not the only tourist confused. The sculpture made me think of a military-like concrete bunker. I even thought about the possibility of a nuclear fallout shelter, and wondered whether it was supposed to be a warning against a contemporary genocide. I read the explanation given in a tourist brochure:

> The memorial ... has the form of a library turned inside out. On the plinth surrounding the memorial are the names of the places were [*sic*] 65,000 Austrian Jews were murdered by the Nazis. (Jewish Museum Vienna 2006, n.p.)

Note the discrepancy in death toll between the brochure and the United States Holocaust Memorial Museum's figures. Whatever the actual number (and numbers are notoriously difficult to ascertain due to the Nazis' destruction of records, the failure to register many prisoners, and the re-allocation of prisoner numbers to new inmates after the original bearer had died), I couldn't see a library, inside out or right side in. Another tourist suggested it was a big garden shed. A third looked for a way in, as she was sure the memorial must be downstairs somewhere. Others just shook their heads, walked around, and shook their heads again. Whatever it was we had come for, none of us seemed to have found it. It made me think of Tumarkin's warning: 'instead of representing the past, [memorials] may in fact mystify and displace it' (2005, p. 204). There was nothing in that memorial that resonated for me in any way with the journalistic or historical records of the time, or with memoirs from survivors. It distanced me rather than brought me closer to what I sought.

I am what Gary Weissman calls a 'nonwitness', one of those who 'have no immediate, familial connection to the Holocaust' (2004, p. 5). He argues that one of the reasons nonwitnesses go to sites related to the Holocaust is our desire to 'experience' what it was really like—albeit vicariously; to make it more 'real'.

> it is the unspoken desire of many people who have no direct experience of the Holocaust but are deeply interested in studying, remembering, and memorializing it. It is a desire to know what it was like to be there, in Nazi Europe; in hiding; at the site of mass shootings; in the ghettos; in the cattle cars; in the concentration camps; in the death camps; in the gas chambers and crematoria. The desire can be satisfied only in fantasy, in fantasies of witnessing the Holocaust for oneself. (Weissman 2004, p. 4)

There is certainly an element of truth to that in my case. I wish to understand the reality of others. By seeing, smelling, touching, walking through one small place in space and history, it makes the incomprehensible scale of what happened more accessible. Whenever I do, I know more than I did before, however incomplete that knowledge is. I can never visit the time; I can visit the place. Like Tumarkin, I believe traumascapes matter. I am a product of a culture which prioritises memorialisation, and that inevitably influences my views and conclusions. While one sculpture could never adequately represent what happened throughout Austria (nor did I expect it to), I had hoped to feel something.

The Judenplatz Museum, near the sculpture, is small; at its heart is an archaeological dig. In 1995, according to the brochure, 'archaeologists found the walls of one of the largest medieval synagogues in Europe underneath Judenplatz.' (Jewish Museum Vienna 2006, n.p.). As well as the remains of the walls, there are a few exhibits relating to the Jewish community in Vienna during the Middle Ages, and computer terminals where visitors can search for information about individual Jewish victims of the Holocaust. I was the only visitor, although another arrived just as I was leaving. I asked the staff about other memorials or museums; they told me to go to Mauthausen. The main part of the Jewish Museum, at the Palais Eskeles, is larger and more popular. It includes a research library, which I did not have time to explore on this trip. The intention behind this visit (officially a holiday) was not to spend time in libraries. It was to discover what would be apparent to other visitors as well as locals: visible, accessible reminders of the past. I wanted to see what was open to the world, not what was segregated for researchers, available within certain times on certain days, behind doors, on library shelves or in filing cabinets. My purpose was to see the places where the past occurred, and to see how it was commemorated. Despite the comparatively small Jewish population now in Vienna, efforts had been made to recognise the impact of Jewish involvement in Austrian life over the centuries, and the impact of the Nazi era on the Jews.

It was not, of course, only the Jews who were pilloried, jailed and killed. Austria had a history of resistance to, as well as support of, Nazism. (Mind you, so had German voters.) That side of history was invisible. It would be difficult, perhaps impossible, to acknowledge

Austrian victims without acknowledging Austrian perpetrators. But implicitly the message is that the atrocities happened to Jews alone, and by the German Nazis rather than Austrians themselves: to 'them', not 'us'; by 'them', not 'us'. As Zygmunt Bauman warns,

> The self-healing of historical memory which occurs in the consciousness of modern society is for this reason more than a neglect offensive to the victims of the genocide. It is also a sign of dangerous and potentially suicidal blindness. (1989, p. x)

Vienna's physical segregation of evidence and commemoration seemed to represent a psychological distancing: a mental veil dividing past and present, an aid to that 'blindness'. People can choose not to see.

According to Roger Boyes (2008), it was precisely that attitude that was highlighted by the infamous Fritzl case. On 29 April 2008, seventy-three-year-old Josef Fritzl confessed to police that he had imprisoned his daughter for twenty-four years, fathering seven children on her, three of which he and his wife raised publicly, while three remained imprisoned in the small, windowless basement from birth. The seventh baby died at birth. His wife and neighbours claimed ignorance of the abuse. The *Times* described that alleged ignorance as 'incredible' (*Australian* 2008, p. 11). Boyes blames not only Josef Frizl, but Austrian officialdom and society in general:

> Austria is a society that nurtures its secrets, that suppresses its history, that blocks out uncomfortable biographies ... it is the interlocking circles of secrecy that make Austria special in the way it deals with, or ignores, individual tragedies ... [Fritzl's] crime was made possible by a society that is inclined to look away rather than experience discomfort. (Boyes 2008, p. 11)

Boyes links the 'look-away' (p. 11) attitudes illustrated by the recent revelations to those demonstrated by Austria's ready absorption of its

Nazis and collaborators into postwar society, and its failure to bring known perpetrators of atrocities to justice.

> The ignoble fact is that 40 per cent of the staff and three-quarters of the commandants of concentration camps were of Austrian origin. It was Austrians, mostly, who organised the deportation of the Jews: 80 per cent of the staff of Adolf Eichmann, the logistics planner of the Holocaust, were from Austria. (p. 11)

The assumption that the Fritzl case and postwar behaviour are linked by a cultural attitude needs to be examined. Austria is not the only nation where terrible crimes have been committed, nor where those crimes have remained undiscovered for some time. Many Austrians did adopt a rabid enthusiasm for Nazism, but this was public. Everyone knew who had been involved, what they had done; even those who may not have been party members themselves were often collaborators or witnesses (particularly because camps were often cheek-by-jowl with their Austrian neighbours, and scores of thousands of prisoners were forced to work in Austrian-owned or -run businesses). This was not a case of collective ignorance (intentional or not), as was the Fritzl case, but collective knowledge. Keeping quiet was likely to be driven by self-protection, loyalty, or the desire to avoid postwar confrontation or punishment. The lack of curiosity about the daughter's disappearance or the sudden arrival of three children on the Fritzl doorstep seems at least peculiar and—in terms of the permitted adoptions without inquiries into the mother's whereabouts—apparently negligent. It seems implausible that nobody noticed, for twenty-four years, what was going on. It does seem plausible that people did not want to get involved. The results may have been the same—enabling secrecy—but it appears to me that there are differences. Fundamentally, though, there is a common thread: an unwillingness to publicly acknowledge the uncomfortable, the unpleasant, the shameful. Whether that is a characteristic that is peculiarly Austrian is debateable; after all, it took until the twenty-first century for the Australian government to formally acknowledge

Figure 3 Mauthausen entrance gates (author's photo)

and apologise for the policies that resulted in generations of Aboriginal children being removed from their families.

Linz, hometown of Adolf Hitler and Adolf Eichmann, nestles in the hills, with steep cobblestoned streets (hazardous in the ice). I kept my eyes open for anything marking the town's intimate connection with Nazism. I expected none, and saw none. Among other things, why would any town want to provide a focus for the neo-Nazi movement? Besides, I'd come to believe what everyone had told me in other cities and towns: Mauthausen was where I would find out about the war in Austria.

The next morning, wearing all my warmest clothes, I caught the bus to Gusen. Mauthausen concentration camp is about two kilometres' walk up the hill from there. There was snowy slush at the side of the road, and some bends were still icy. The breeze came straight from the snow-covered mountains. I was lucky; part-way up the road a taxi stopped and I was able to save myself a walk. While relieved to be in the warmth, there was an element of guilt—I was taking the easy way out. I was being a privileged tourist, not a serious nonwitness; how could I perceive even slightly what conditions would be like for a prisoner when I so quickly took advantage of any comfort that came my way? I had the justifications of a bad cold and a lack of time, but still ... there was a sense of 'serves me right' when I discovered I had dropped a glove in the taxi while paying the fare. My coat had no pockets. By the time I had walked to the main gates, a matter of minutes, the back of my hand was a patchy white and red and the knuckles were aching. My breath frosted the air. I was ready to go in.

Visiting a memorial, camp or museum can prove disappointing and alienating; it may, in fact, have the reverse effect than that sought. My experiences in Vienna highlighted that. But walking through a place where horrors and cruelty occurred makes them more real; by personally recognising the place, I can 'see' the events more clearly. Mauthausen houses a museum, but it is also a memorial in its own right. It's where it happened, not just a place where we can find out what happened. It is where my nonwitness fantasy to understand was most likely to be met.

Looking down from the top of Mauthausen's Staircase of Death (which leads to the quarry; both sites of many deaths), of tackling steps in icy conditions, gives me some idea of what it would have been like for those incarcerated and killed there. I can extrapolate and imagine: I was cold despite coat, scarf, boots and hat; they wore cotton uniforms and whatever else they could scrounge. I was worried about slipping or my arthritic knees giving out, so walked gingerly, one step at a time; they were forced to run, all day, carrying awkward, oppressively-heavy rocks. Mauthausen primarily housed political prisoners; these intellectuals, artists, writers, educated men (women were not inmates of the camp until September 1944), probably would have been as little practised in physical labour as I am. I did not have to worry about being pushed off the edge as a 'parachuter' (the ironic term for those who fell, jumped or were pushed to their deaths in the quarry below), or falling on other prisoners and causing their deaths. I didn't have to worry about the guards and beatings and guns and dogs; only of getting the bus back to Linz in time to catch my train. My experience was petty and incomplete, and made me feel very small in trying to capture anything—even imaginatively—of what others lived; *but it was not vicarious.* It made the stories and reports and histories real in a way that reading alone does not, however horrific the reading. Take this report on the experiences of the first group of Jewish men from Amsterdam to be sent to Mauthausen, arriving on 17 June 1941:

> A batch of fifty was immediately killed: 'They were chased naked from the bathhouse to the electrified fence.' The others were murdered in the main quarry of the camp, the 'Vienna ditch.' According to the German witness Eugen Kogon, these Jews were not allowed to use the steps leading to the bottom of the quarry. 'They had to slide down the loose stones at the side, and even here many died or were severely injured. The survivors then had to shoulder hods, and two prisoners were compelled to load each Jew with an excessively heavy rock. The Jews then had to run up the 186 steps. In some instances the rocks immediately rolled downhill, crushing the feet of those that came behind. Every Jew who lost his rock in that fashion was brutally beaten, and the rock was hoisted onto his shoulders again. Many of the Jews were driven to despair the very first day and committed suicide by jumping into the pit. On the third day the SS opened the so-called 'death gate,' and with a fearful barrage of blows drove the Jews across the guard line, the guards on the watchtowers shooting them down in heaps with their machine guns. The next day the Jews no longer jumped into the pit individually. They joined hands and one man would pull nine or twelve of his comrades over the lip with him into a gruesome death. The barracks were 'cleared' of Jews, not in six but in barely three weeks. Every one of the 348 prisoners perished by suicide, or by shooting, beating, and other forms of torture. (Horwitz, cited in Friedlander 2007, p. 181)

In the two Mauthausen war crimes trials following the war (1946 and 1947), sixty-nine people were accused of crimes including murder, torture, beating and starving the inmates. The accused included several doctors, as well as kapos, guards and administrators. Only one was acquitted; fifty-three were hanged for their crimes and the others imprisoned. The death toll of inmates at Mauthausen and its sub-camps will never be known precisely, estimates range between 122 766 (the total cited on a stone tablet at Mauthausen, erected by Austrian authorities) and 320 000 (by Wnuk 1961, cited in Wikipedia)

Of course, not all perpetrators were called to account. Nazi-hunter Efraim Zuroff announced in 2008 that 'Dr Death'—'the most wanted Nazi war criminal still believed to be alive' (Reuters, 2008 p. 13)—was thought to be hiding in southern Chile. Aribert Heim was an Austrian doctor at Mauthausen who allegedly removed organs from inmates without using anaesthetic, and killed hundreds by injecting their hearts with petrol or poison and timed their deaths with a stopwatch. There were plans to prosecute him in Germany in 1962, but he fled. He is now in his nineties, and Zuroff warned that he may die before he

Figure 4 Mauthausen plaques (author's photo)

is discovered and forced to stand trial, 'something which we find to be a travesty of justice' (Reuters 2008, p. 13). Heim's family claims he died in 1993.

Knowing of at least some of the cruelties and murders that took place at Mauthausen, I was seeking the personal as well as the collective stories. Both were there, at least in part.

As well as the national monuments to victims that line the road near the camp, plaques have been placed along the camp wall, overlooked by watchtowers and barbed wire. They give a partial picture of the range of people who suffered and died here. Some show the Star of David, but many do not. For the first time, I felt that victims' voices which had been silent—the political prisoners, the Soviet prisoners of war, the Jehovah's Witnesses, the homosexuals, the Romany, the partisans—were being recognised. In my research, I look at whose stories are being told, and whose are not: who, effectively, has been removed from the Holocaust story? The variety of nationalities, beliefs and activities of victims represented in plaque after plaque helped show how wide-ranging the Nazi oppression had been. It would be impossible for any visitor to ignore the fact that as well as the six million Jewish victims, there were millions of others who suffered and died at the hands of the regime. Not all concentration camps had the variety of inmates of Mauthausen, of course, but that the scope of victims was acknowledged here was a relief. There were still gaps and silences. The barracks were not open to tourists due to storm damage a few years earlier; they were trying to raise money for their restoration. In the meantime, the damage was getting worse.

But the lack of translations in the museum was what struck me most. Everything was in German; yet on the day I visited the overwhelming majority of people were foreigners, most of us English-speakers. I missed the significance of some exhibits, many of which were documents. Space for translations would be tight (and raises questions of which languages should be included), but I had expected some kind of photocopied handout with information, however limited. It felt as if they did not want us to know—a foolishly personal response, no doubt, but a reflection of what I had increasingly begun to believe in my time in Austria. A Spanish family with English as their second language commented on how hard it was for them to work out the displays. They had come to Austria specifically to see Mauthausen; former Republican fighters from the Spanish Civil War had been incarcerated and killed there. There was a memorial just off the approach road, which I was able to direct them to; like them, I did not know that English guidebooks were sold at the entry gates until I was leaving. They had not been displayed when we arrived; they had to be requested. My suspicions in the museum seemed excessive, but not entirely unfounded.

What moved me—gave me the emotional as well as intellectual response I had sought throughout my Austrian journey—was far less official than these plaques or museum exhibits, though. In one of the gas chambers—much smaller than I had expected—the grief of those left behind was palpable. Family photos of those who had died, along with messages from the bereaved, were stuck to the walls. Individuals were named, pictured and mourned. The messages came from friends, fellow resistance members and trade unionists, wives and lovers, siblings and children and parents. Some messages were faded, the photos slightly worn, as if often handled and deeply cherished before they were placed on these walls. Others looked more recent, better preserved, professionally printed. As with the plaques, they were in many languages, and sometimes I could only understand a symbol, name or dates. There were pink triangles, red hammers and sickles, yellow stars, crosses, to name a few. Each individual named and missed represented so many more. The sense of loss reinforced that it was not simply about the numbers and scale of the killings; it was that each one was an individual, that each had a family, friends, whose lives would never be the same without them. It was personal. I resented the intrusion of other visitors, their conversations, their casual glancing at some messages and ignoring of others. I felt

Figure 5 Plaque for homosexual victims at Mauthausen (author's photo)

compelled to look at all. When a man asked some others to be quiet, I was relieved. Their chattering felt sacrilegious. They left; more arrived. The man and I both walked out in silence. The shrine had become a tourist attraction, and we did not want to be associated with tourists. It may be a paradox, considering we were tourists, too—but it seemed like there was a difference in attitude; we thought of ourselves as nonwitnesses, witnessing rather than tourists on a day trip. I needed to get outside, breathe deeply in the cold, and feel space and silence around me. I needed to absorb what I had seen, and remember my feelings. I went back to the plaques, thinking of some of the individuals pictured that I could now associate with particular memorials. The plaques felt more 'real' and personal, less formal now.

Those who lived close to the camp also took it personally at times. However, it was in a completely different way:

> On September 27, 1941, Eleanore Gusenbauer sent a letter of complaint to the Mauthausen police station: 'In the concentration camp Mauthausen at the work site in Vienna Ditch inmates are being shot repeatedly; those badly struck live for yet some time, and so remain lying next to the dead for hours or even half a day long. My property lies upon an elevation next to the Vienna Ditch, and one is often an unwilling witness to such outrages. I am anyway sickly and such a sight makes a demand on my nerves that in the long run I cannot bear. I request that it be arranged that such inhuman deeds be discontinued, *or else done where one does not see it*'. (in Friedlander 2007, p. 295; my italics)

In this situation, the temptation to make a judgement of a whole culture—to extrapolate—is strong. As Schlink states, Hannah Arendt, in writing about Eichmann's trial, said

> Since the whole of respectable society had in one way or another succumbed to Hitler, the moral maxims which determine social behaviour and the religious commandments—'Thou shalt not kill!'—which guide conscience had virtually vanished. (2005, p. 125)

Her argument is that in allocating collective guilt, individual guilt is harder to pinpoint; Schlink concurs, saying in relation to Germany's recognition of collective guilt after the war, 'whilst acknowledging everyone's guilt and seeking forgiveness for all, they neglected to renounce individual perpetrators and participants (2009, p. 16). Both Schlink (2009) and Arendt (2005) discuss judgement and justice as they relate to what happened during the war, and how humanity makes up its mind after the events. Arendt is scathing about the conduct, focus and procedures of the Israeli trial of Adolf Eichmann in 1961. Schlink is more circumspect about the effect of contemporary recognition and judgements of the past, pointing to some of the dangers resulting from his generation's 'preoccupation with the Third Reich and the Holocaust' (2009, p. 30).

Questions of responsibility, guilt and blame, of how we assess and interpret actions, inactions and events, are never simple. While the actions of a person like 'Dr Death' may clearly be determined as evil, what of those like Gusenbauer? She did not pull a trigger, and had even asked for the 'inhuman deeds' to be stopped, but her alternative request—that the killings take place where she could not see them—makes her in my mind still guilty of complicity. The smear attached to her behaviour is moral, not legal. She knew, but did not want to see. When the camp was liberated in 1945, local residents were forced to remove inmates' bodies for burial. The US officers and soldiers had no hesitation in making them share responsibility for the cruelties at Mauthausen. Perhaps that is where the 'resentment' that Edinger (2009) identified in contemporary Austria really began.

Fear of association with those whose actions could be punishable by law may have been a motive for silence in postwar Austria, as may a collective resentment about being on the losing side of the war, but what about since? Doesn't the community desire not to see, not to remember, enable perpetrators to abrogate responsibility? If those who were legally punishable do not need to take responsibility, then why should others less guilty—or, in their minds (as I'm sure Gusenbauer thought of herself) those not guilty at all? After all, they argue, Austria was invaded by the Germans—what choice did they have? The justifying and self-distancing, the rejection of responsibility, appears unchanged over the generations. Nazi rather than Austrian actions are acknowledged at Mauthausen; by implication, 'Nazi' equates to 'German'. The camp and museum clearly acknowledge that terrible deeds took place on Austrian soil, but—again—the implicit message is that the perpetrators were 'them', not 'us'.

While writing this chapter, I have repeatedly listened to Mikis Theodorakis' 'The Ballad of Mauthausen'. The lyrics were written by Mauthausen survivor Iakovos Kambanellis. He based his 'Song of Songs' on the photograph of an unknown woman, a photo he discovered at Mauthausen and kept with him. Through his lyrics, the personal and collective loss, the individual and the representative of so many, are intimately intertwined:

How beautiful my love is
In her everyday dress
And a little comb in her hair
No-one knew how beautiful she is

Young girls of Auschwitz
Young girls of Dachau
Have you seen my love?
We saw her on a long journey
She no longer had her dress
Nor the little comb in her hair

How beautiful my love is
The caress of her mother
And the kisses of her brother
No-one knew how beautiful she is

Young girls of Mauthausen
Young girls of Belsen
Have you seen my love?
We saw her in the frozen square
With a number on her white arm
With a yellow star on her heart

How beautiful my love is
The caress of her mother
And the kisses of her brother
No-one knew how beautiful she is

The song, like the personal photos and messages in the gas chamber, connects me to the larger loss, the scale of which is otherwise incomprehensible. Walking and looking and touching and considering Mauthausen did, in some ways at least, bring the fantasy of understanding a little nearer. But it also reinforced the stereotype of Austrian attitudes, their 'look-away' culture and narrative repositioning. It is a traumascape only partly acknowledged, in a country which has corralled this part of its past to one site, important as it is. For Austrians and tourists alike, it takes a deliberate effort to visit—and nationally, it appears to encourage the idea that the cruelties of the Nazi era were also taking place away from view, instead of in the streets of every town, in full sight of Austrians.

I partly agree with Schlink's argument:

> A collective past, like that of an individual, is traumatic when it is not allowed to be remembered, and is just as much so if it has to be remembered ... Detraumatisation is the process of becoming able to both remember and forget; it is leaving the past in the past, in a way that embraces remembrance as well as forgetting. This applies in the same way to the victims and their descendants as to the perpetrators and their descendents. (2009, p. 36)

If he intends 'forgetting' to mean moving on to a new understanding and vision for a society once the past is remembered and responsibility acknowledged, then I support his view. Yet what is being remembered in Austria, where and how? Who is presented as being responsible for the events of the past? It was not so much the layers of the past I discovered, as a single site presented ambiguously. As a nonwitness bred in a culture of memorialising traumascapes, I cannot help questioning such a poor national memory, and feeling that detraumamatisation or reconciliation with the past will never occur while acknowledgement remains so partial.

Notes

1. < http://www.gusen.org/>
2. < http://www.gusen.org/dok/hmann01x.htm>
3. *Shoah* is the Hebrew term for the Holocaust.

References

Arendt, H 2005, *Eichmann and the Holocaust*, Penguin Books, London.

Australian 2008, 'Dungeon father had sex assault conviction', 30 April, p. 11.

Bauman, Z 1989, *Modernity and the Holocaust*, Cornell University Press, Ithaca, New York.

Boyes, R 2008, 'In Austria, no one can hear you scream', *Australian*, 30 April, p. 11.

Clendinnen, I 1998, *Reading the Holocaust*, Text Publishing, Melbourne.

Edinger, H 2009, *Voices on Anti-Semitism*, podcast, United States Holocaust Memorial Museum, viewed 27 May 2009, <http://www.ushmm.org/museum/exhibit/focus/ antisemitism/voices/ transcript/ ?content=20090101)>.

Farantouri, M n.d. *Song of Songs*, accessed 28 May 2009, <http://www.imeem.com/people/pKqP-0/music/JuIDow04/maria-farantouri-greeceasma-asmaton-song-of-songs-live-v/>.

Friedlander, S 2007, *The Years of Extermination: Nazi Germany and the Jews 1939 – 1945*, HarperCollins Publishers, New York.

Gusen Memorial Committee, viewed 25 May 2009, < http://www.gusen.org/>.

Hammelmann , J 1998, trans. S Witzany-Durda & J White, *Preface*, KZ Mauthausen-GUSEN Info-Pages, viewed 25 May 2009, <http://www.gusen.org/dok/hmann 01x.htm> .

Hoffman, E 2004, *After Such Knowledge: Memory, history and the legacy of the Holocaust*, PublicAffairs, Perseus Books, Cambridge, MA.

Jewish Museum Vienna 2006, *One Museum, Two Houses*, Judisches Museum der Stadt Wien GmbH, Vienna.

Langer, L 1982 *Versions of Survival: The Holocaust and the Human Spirit*, State University of New York Press, Albany.

Liberation of Mauthausen 1945, film, viewcd 20 July 2009, <http://www.ushmm.org/wlc/media_fi.php?lang=en&ModuleId=10005196&MediaId=213>.

Marsalek, H (ed.) 1996, Mauthausen 8.8.1938 – 5.5.1945, Osterreichische Lagergemeinschaft Mauthausen, Vienna, < http://www.gusen.org/>.

Mauthausen-Gusen Concentration Camp, Wikipedia, viewed 29 May 2009, <http://en.wikipedia.org/wiki/Mauthausen-Gusen_concentration_camp>.

Morse, AD 1968, *While Six Million Died*, Martin Secker & Warburg, London.

Reuters 2008, 'Nazi hunter narrows search for 'Dr Death', *Australian*, 21 May, p. 13.

Schlink, B 2009, *Guilt about the Past*, University of Queensland Press, St Lucia, Qld.

Shirer, WL 1984, *The Nightmare Years 1930 – 1940*, Bantam Books, New York.

Theodorakis, M 1966 *The Ballad of Mauthausen*, lyrics by Iakovos Kambanellis, Colombia Records.

Tumarkin, M 2005, *Traumascapes*, Melbourne University Press, Victoria.

United States Holocaust Memorial Museum, viewed 24 May 2009, <http://www.ushmm.org/>.

Weissman, G 2004, *Fantasies of Witnessing: Postwar Efforts to Experience the Holocaust.*, Cornell University Press, Ithaca, NY.

Chapter 5

Power in paradise: How Queensland's north opposed the Japanese advance

Kerry Green
University of South Australia

Although World War 2's Pacific campaigns barely touched Australia's shores, they nevertheless left a deep and permanent mark on the country. Australians of all ages are well acquainted with the attack on Sydney by Japanese midget submarines and many are also aware of the tremendous damage inflicted on Darwin by Japanese bombing raids. But the war left other marks—marks which are unknown to most Australians today. Most Australians, for example, would be unaware of the major wartime role played by Cairns and its hinterland, in the north of Queensland. Huge numbers of troops and wartime materiel—Australian and American—flowed through this region as the Allies struggled to respond to Japanese attacks.

Cairns residents do, in fact, know their wartime history. Indeed, if you visit the region, it is impossible to ignore the relics of war, still so obvious more than sixty years after the end of the conflict. Cairns International Airport, like so much else in Cairns, exists because US forces drained the surrounding swamps to improve the rudimentary airstrip. Whole suburbs are on former swamp land drained by 'the Yanks', and some of the massive wharves through which so much commerce still flows likewise owe their existence to the US forces.

What is not so obvious, however, is evidence of the huge numbers of units that flowed through the Cairns hinterland, into the Atherton and Evelyn Tablelands, during World War 2. According to some reports, the units camped west of Cairns comprised the biggest concentration of troops anywhere in Australia. Some estimates put the number of troops at any one time as high as 100 000. Cairns historian Vera Bradley (n.d.) quotes a figure of 80 000 on the Cairns Museum website, but an Atherton Shire Council publication puts the figure at between 200 000 and 300 000. Certainly, the Rocky Creek Field Hospital, halfway between the towns of Mareeba and Atherton, is recognised as the biggest military hospital in Australia during the war.

The units brought with them all the energy, economic development, activity and tragedy of the war. It was here a unit commander reported his wife's suspicions of sedition, sparking an inquiry followed by a death; it was here an accidental bomb explosion killed two soldiers and wounded dozens more, and it was from here that Australian and US airmen flew countless combat missions against Japanese forces to the north, sometimes never to return.

With the exception of Rocky Creek, which has been developed into a magnificent memorial park, little has been done to acknowledge the role this part of Australia—then, as now, remote from the main centres of population—played in the successful prosecution of the war in the Pacific.

The Atherton and Evelyn Tablelands played a crucial role in the Allies' war effort. Like Cairns, they were close enough to Papua New Guinea and islands to the north to provide a convenient staging post for troops entering or leaving the battlefield, but unlike Cairns on the coast, remote enough and sufficiently hidden in the bushland to be safe from shelling and bombing raids. Indeed, when the danger of Japanese invasion became apparent, civilians in Cairns were evacuated to the tablelands for safety. General Thomas Blamey is reported (National Servicemen's Association of Australia, Qld (NSAA)) to have investigated the hinterland to the west of Cairns and found it to be an ideal region for a 'tropical training ground and rehabilitation area'. 'For one brief period between September and November 1944, all three AIF divisions (6th, 7th and 9th) were on the Tableland at one time,' the source says.

Figure 1 Memorial to the Japanese bombing of Mossman, north of Cairns (author's photo)

The war was more than just a distant conflict for the people of Far North Queensland; Japanese bombers attacked Townsville three times (with notable lack of success), and a Japanese flying boat dropped a bomb which exploded near a house outside of Mossman, north of Cairns, injuring a child. In recent years, Far Northerners have come to recognise the need to record events of the war years, and on the fiftieth anniversary of the Mossman bombing a plaque was erected on the site. In the bald language of bureaucratese, it notes:

> JAPANESE AIR RAID ON DOUGLAS SHIRE—1942
>
> At 3.30am on 31/7/42, a Japanese aircraft dropped eight bombs in this shire, one landing fifty metres directly behind this point. Carmel Zullo, aged 2 ½ years, was asleep in the home of her parents when

> the bomb exploded nearby. Shrapnel pierced the iron walls of the house, one fragment grazing Carmel's skull. She was the only civilian casualty inflicted by the enemy on the eastern Australian mainland throughout World War 2.

Happily, on 31 July 1992, fifty years after the attack, it was Carmel Emmi (nee Zullo) who unveiled the memorial to the raid which could have so easily killed her.

Contemporary reports tell of fears that Japanese submarines had landed spies along the long and largely undefended coastline. Cairns historian Vera Bradley (1995, p. 169) reports Anglican bishop Arthur Malcolm saying he and a group of other boys encountered Japanese soldiers surveying the area around Yarrabah Mission, south of Cairns, for example. She also cites coastwatcher Eric McGuffie's anger over official inaction following his reports of Japanese submarines regularly landing parties on the Queensland coast in 1942–43.

The military sites to the west of Cairns, therefore, assumed great significance, with airfields providing launching pads for US and Australian planes attacking Japanese forces in Papua New Guinea and in the Coral Sea, and huge campsites providing training settings and staging posts for troops heading for battle.

Bradley notes on the Cairns Museum website (n.d.):

> The people of Cairns began a rapid change of lifestyle. Education in Far North Queensland was first affected, as the Queensland Government ordered all schools in North Queensland to close. Civilians were strongly advised to evacuate to the south. Special passes had to be issued to all residents who lived north of Tully [about 90 minutes south of Cairns by road]. A blackout system and air raid alarms were also introduced, and aircraft spotters watched the skies for enemy aircraft. Old dray tracks that had lain unused for over 60 years were brushed up and local guides were trained to show civilians

where these tracks were in the event of evacuation. This was because the only ways out of Cairns until the middle of 1942 were the Cairns-Herberton railway line and the Gillies Highway.

Visitors to World War 2 military sites on the tablelands necessarily have an imperfect knowledge of the enormous activity and economic development that went on here during the war years. Service clubs and RSLs have signposted many of the major sites, but the signs give no indication of the sheer size of the unit campsites.

On the other hand, some of the most obvious reminders of wartime development go unnoticed in the very middle of suburbia. Mareeba airport, an hour west of Cairns by road, is an example. Built by US troops, it was home to B-17 Flying Fortresses and long-range Avro Anson reconnaissance planes, among others; General MacArthur flew in here, in a Flying Fortress, on an inspection tour. War planes still fly out of Mareeba Airport, a busy general aviation site, but now instead of carrying bombs the planes of Warbird Adventures carry tourists keen to experience what it was like to fly a P-40 Kittyhawk or a DC3.

The missions of the US and Australian airmen stationed at Mareeba are outlined in Damian Waters' book, *Beaus, Butchers and Boomerangs* (2003), which follows the many triumphs and tragedies, adventures and escapades of the crews who flew sorties out of Mareeba. Waters notes in his Introduction (p. 7) that the passage of time makes the achievement of strict accuracy a difficult task. That difficulty is reinforced in Bradley's book, *I Didn't Know That* (1995), in which she refers to persistent accounts of the Mareeba planes participating in the Battle of the Coral Sea. That battle, thousands of kilometres to the east of Cairns, was fought exclusively between carrier-borne US and Japanese planes, and the units at Mareeba were never involved. Likewise, reports that the residents of Cairns could hear the 'gunfire' of the battle were similarly fanciful. Nor were such flights of fancy required: there was more than enough real death and disaster—and selfless sacrifice—to go around.

Figure 2 Merriland Hall in Atherton, one of the largest military igloos in Australia, has served the community in a variety of capacities—including playing host to famous symphony orchestras (author's photo)

An even more obvious and just as unremarked relic of the war years is Merriland Hall, in the centre of Atherton's Showground, half an hour south of Mareeba. Merriland Hall is the classic army 'igloo', or parabolic arch. The original US design called for camouflage netting covering, but in Queensland the igloos were clothed in corrugated iron. Merriland is a big igloo—originally 200 feet by 100 feet (approximately 60 x 30 metres), but expanded over the years; it is one of very few large igloos still standing on their original wartime sites. Built to provide a canteen and housing a bakery which supplied bread to all the units in the region, Merriland has been listed with the Queensland government as a place of significant cultural heritage.

Merriland might have provided bread to soldiers in the war years, but it has provided much more than that in the following years. It has been a show pavilion, a shire hall, a community centre and a cultural centre. The Australian and Queensland ballets have performed here, as has the Queensland Symphony Orchestra. Today, Merriland Hall serves the community as a theatre, community centre and dance hall; while it is undoubtedly iconic, it has become such a central part of Atherton's life that its wartime provenance is largely unremarked, despite its proximity to the drill hall of 51 Battalion, Far North Queensland regiment.

The most obvious and evocative wartime relic is the Rocky Creek Memorial Park. According to NSAA the hospital complex, which stretches both sides of the Kennedy Highway, was

> the largest in the southern hemisphere, with a 5000-bed capacity and 2000 staff. Those patients that died of wounds or sickness are buried in the 164 graves at the Atherton War Cemetery that is maintained by the Commonwealth War Graves Commission.

Rocky Creek Memorial Park commemorates the work of the 2/2nd and 2/6th Army General Hospital and associated units, which from 1943 until the end of the war treated more than 60 000 patients, most of whom came by ship from Papua New Guinea to Cairns and were then transported by 'ambulance train' to Rocky Creek (Atherton Shire Council, n.d.). Tranter and Tranter (2003, p. 3) note:

> When Australian troops were poised for imminent battles in New Guinea all hospitals would be alerted for new casualties, moving as many patients as possible to southern hospitals by ambulance train.

The ambulance trains themselves performed amazing feats of mass movement, transporting more than 230 patients at a time from the far north of Queensland to Toowoomba and Warwick, more than 1600 km away in the far south over a period of three days, at an average speed of 40 km/h. Tranter and Tranter (2003, p. 19) quote Sister Nan McCallum, who made the trip many times during 1943:

> One remembers the kindliness and friendliness of the railway staff along the way ... The stationmaster at Rockhampton always opened the hot showers for us, even at 3am. To be able to indulge in the luxury of a hot shower while the train was revictualled and visited by Red Cross personnel was a great boon ... When the president of the local Red Cross Society invited us all to a Red Cross Ball in the town, an incredible number of patient recoveries took place.

Rocky Creek has inspired memories nostalgic, tragic and comic in those who served or recuperated there. Some of the comic tales involve a character called Mortuary Mitch, the hospital's undertaker. Nurses Dawn Walker and Pansy Hood reminisce about Mortuary Mitch in Tranter and Tranter (2003, pp. 52–53). One of the tales involves Mortuary Mitch when he was serving with the hospital in the Middle East. A body was being transported in the back of an ambulance and Mitch decided he would hitch a ride. Dawn Walker takes up the story:

> He didn't have time to contact the ambulance driver and as the ambulance started up, Mitch yelled and ran after it. The driver didn't hear him, but Mitch managed to grab the tailboard and hauled himself in. As far as the driver knew, there was only the corpse in the back. So the three were trundling along in the desert, when Mitch suddenly put his head out of the back curtain, and projected his voice into the driver's window, yelling, 'Take the next turn to the right mate, it's shorter.' Well, the driver nearly had a heart attack, took the turn to the right, and slammed the vehicle into a palm tree. No one was hurt, least of all the corpse, but what the driver said to Mitch when he discovered the extra passenger in the back does not bear repeating.

But the Rocky Creek Hospital did much more than contribute to Australian war folklore. Apart from the countless lives saved by the tireless efforts of the medical staff, research conducted at the hospital also had a significant effect on the treatment and prevention

Figure 3 Mounted plaques commemorate the work of individual units at the Rocky Creek Hospital Memorial Park, near Tolga on the Atherton Tableland. Cairns resident Fred Gong, whose parents both served during World War 2, checks the unit names. (author's photo)

of malaria, showing that the drug Atebrin was more useful than quinine. This is a site where Australians fought a different kind of battle—a battle to mend broken bodies and minds, and visitors to the hospital site, which is continually being developed, cannot help but be impressed by it.

An hour west and south of Rocky Creek lies a clutch of small towns like Herberton and Ravenshoe, which played host to huge concentrations of units training for war in the Pacific. The sites of these huge camps are marked by signs pointing off the Kennedy Highway, leading west from the coast over the top of the Great Dividing Range. A publication produced by the Atherton Tableland Information Centre notes (n.d.):

> The 6th Division occupied an area on the Wondecla-Ravenshoe Road and the theatre still stands to this day. The 7th Division camped on the Ravenshoe-Mt Garnet Road following their return from New Guinea ... Various places were out of bounds, one of which was Bones Knob, where there used to be an ammunition depot, with part of the hill honeycombed for the safe storage of ammunition.

Ironically, it was at one of the camps that a Japanese rifle grenade did its deadly work, killing two and injuring fifty-three when it rolled off a table and exploded during a demonstration at Wondecla, near Herberton (2/6th Cavalry Commando Regiment, n.d.).

Wondecla also was the site of a possible case of sedition, recounted by Dr Kevin Baker (2006, pp. 195–196). In 1943, new battalion commander Colonel Paul Cullen is visited at Wondecla by 'a local Englishman' who 'dropped in to see the new arrivals' and was duly invited to a mess dinner. Various pleasantries followed, leading to a visit by the colonel's wife to the Englishman's grand home in the bush, where 'she became increasingly suspicious of her host's bona fides' (2006, p. 196).

> Mrs Cullen conveyed her suspicions to her husband, who went to the Englishman's house in his absence. With mixed feelings about abuse of hospitality and patriotism, Cullen searched through the Englishman's desk and discovered some concealed compartments, which were only accessible when the desk was pulled out from the wall. There he found considerable correspondence in German and English relating to his duties as a representative of the Third Reich. The documents referred to taking control of the roads, the railway station at Atherton, and other vital installations on the Tableland ...

> Colonel Cullen handed over the documents he had collectd to 6th Division Headquarters Intelligence Section. Shortly afterwards, the Englishman became very ill, went to hospital in Herberton and died within two or three days.

Atherton Shire Council has done a great job of marking the camp sites of the various units, but the Englishman's home has not yet been definitively identified—it could be one of a number of imposing stone residences in the district. Nevertheless, at the achingly beautiful Millstream Falls, at Ravenshoe, visitors can walk a historical interpretive trail that takes them through one of the camps and explains what the remnants represent. The soldiers who lived and trained here might have been thousands of kilometres from home, but they did so in one of Queensland's most beautiful bush settings.

Figure 4 *Many Australian units trained near Ravenshoe. Local authorities with the help of the RSL have marked their camp sites for visitors. This sign is on the Kennedy Highway, between Ravenshoe and Mt Garnet. (author's photo)*

Figure 5 *An interpretive trail at the Millstream Falls camp site of 9th Division units passes by a machinegun pit. (author's photo)*

Herberton also is the little-known last resting place of the priest who is believed to have led the first dawn service on 25 April 1923, in Albany, Western Australia. The Reverand Arthur White died in Herberton in 1954 and, as the *Cairns Post* reported, 'a national call has been made ... to build a memorial to the war padre and founder of the dawn service' (2008). The *Cairns Post* reported:

> During World War 1, Mr White set up makeshift chapels on the frontline in France to minister to the troops and the Lions Club wants to build a memorial that resembles one of the tents.

World War 2 brought overwhelming military and economic activity to Far North Queensland and the examples recounted here are just a few of the thousands that still live in the memories of local residents. And to this day, farmers whose fields used to be firing ranges still plough up ordnance requiring specialist disposal. More importantly, the war opened up this part of Australia to investment and development, with many fortunes made (and some lost) as a result. The evidence of that wartime activity and investment is everywhere in Far North Queensland and, while there are many stories still to be told, this is a good time and place to acknowledge the work of Cairns historian Vera Bradley, who recorded a good part of the Far North's wartime history in a number of publications, but most famously in her book *I Didn't Know That*. She died this year—vale Vera Bradley!

References

2/6th Cavalry Commando Regiment (n.d.), 'Wondecla Bomb (The Facts)', viewed 14 November 2008), <www.26cavcommando.org.au>.

Rocky Creek War Memorial Park (n.d.), Atherton Shire Council brochure, Queensland.

War Sites & Markers throughout the Atherton Tablelands region (n.d.), Atherton Shire Council, brochure, Queensland.

Baker, K 2006, *Mutiny, Terrorism, Riots and Murder*, Rosenberg, Sydney.

Bradley, V, 'Defence' Cairns Museum website, viewed 14 November 2008, <http://www.cairnsmuseum.org.au/defence.htm>

Bradley, V 1995, *I Didn't Know That*, Boolarong, Brisbane.

Cairns Post 2008, 'Forgotten Anzac', 24 April, viewed 14 November 2008, <www.cairns.com.au/article/2008/04/24/3361_print-version.html>.

Tranter, H & E 2003, *Remembering Rocky Creek WWII*, Eacham Historical Society, Malanda.

Waters, D 2003, *Beau's, Butchers and Boomerangs: Mareeba, The History of a WWII Airfield 1942-1945*, self-published, Brisbane.

Chapter 6

Biography of the Dinkums—men of Mitcham Camp

Claire Woods
University of South Australia

> The webs of significance of any event, place or person are fine-lined and faint. It takes a lot of looking to see them. (Dening 1998, p. 208)

> What after all, are objects and appearances but stories in disguise. Is not the most mundane of things crystallized history? (Hauser 2008, p. 55)

Introduction

'The street conducts the *flâneur* into a vanished time' (Benjamin 1982; 1999, p. 416). Benjamin's *flâneur* strolls the streets of Paris 'long and aimlessly', whereas I step purposefully along the footpaths of Colonel Light Gardens, a model planned residential suburb lying just south of the City of Adelaide. As a researcher, I am perhaps the 'passionate *flâneur*' redefined for the purpose of tracing and attempting to re-create a past for these streets: a past of almost 100 years ago. In the years 1914–1918, these streets were the site of the Mitcham Army Camp, the staging post for some 50 000 men who volunteered for service in the Australian Imperial Force (AIF) during the First World War. In particular, the focus in this paper is the experience of the men of the 27th Battalion, a home-grown South Australian unit, first raised in February 1915 and whose members' early days in the army were spent at the Mitcham Camp, where their army lives began, their transformation to soldiers was made.

Benjamin, in the dramatic text *Das Passagen-Werk* (The Arcades Project), collected and created a collage of materials to construct a portrait of nineteenth-century Paris, and through this offered a commentary on the social, economic and cultural milieu of the turn of the nineteenth century and the early twentieth century. The translators of a recent edition describe the text and Benjamin's process as a 'display', an 'organised mass of historical objects' (Eiland & McLaughlin, in Benjamin 2002, p. x). These 'objects' are literary excerpts, historical passages, photographs, notes, letters and commentaries, which together create 'an *image* of that epoch' (2002, p. x). In one sense this, then radical form (it was begun in 1927 and the process of collation continued over the next twenty-three years), is a workbook for a biography of a city. One is reminded of Peter Ackroyd's *London: The Biography* (2003). Ackroyd inhabits London with a passionate eye and ear for the city as a living, breathing entity. On the evidence, he would no doubt concur with Tilley, who writes:

> Places, like persons, have biographies inasmuch as they are formed, used and transformed in relation to practice. It can be argued that stories acquire part of their mythic value and historical relevance if they are rooted in the concrete details of locales in the landscape, acquiring material reference points that can be visited, seen and touched. (1994, p. 33)

This paper focuses on a part of the story of the men of an AIF battalion, linking them to places familiar to them in their time. In this sense, it travels the ground not only of place but also of biography, collective biography. It combines the process of walking the ground (the *flâneur* in action) and of gathering from sources and fragments (diaries, newspaper accounts, historical record) those matters which together can build a portrait of people in a certain time and place. The process I describe is aligned not only with a particular contemporary process of '*flânerie*' but also of biographical inquiry in the way biographer Richard Holmes explains:

> 'Biography' meant a book about someone's life. Only for me, it was to become a kind of pursuit, a tracing of the physical trail of someone's path through the past, a following of footsteps. (1995, p. 27)

It is the footsteps of the men of the 27th that I follow here. 'Why should this matter?', the reader might ask. One presumes that the present residents of leafy Colonel Light Gardens are ignorant of the past beneath their feet. Yet, throughout Australia, there are annual rituals, which bear witness to that past and to the men who lent their life experiences to the narratives of Australia. On several particular days, Australians, young and old are asked to seek an affinity and an understanding of their past as written in the lives of the men and women who are their parents, great grandparents, aunts and uncles, brothers and sisters, friends and distant relatives. They gather at war memorials in city parks or streets or in cemeteries in Europe or Asia in commemoration, inhabiting briefly a space and time in contemporary life to make a link with the past.

ANZAC Day (25 April) is the main commemoration of the service and sacrifice of men and women in the wars in which the country has been involved. Armistice Day, 11 November 1918, the day World War I ended is another, memorialised thereafter as Remembrance Day.

****

Remembrance Day, 11 November 2008

Ninety years have elapsed. 'The Greatest Day in History', according to the London *Daily Express* at the time (Best 2008). In 2008, the *Age* editorial opines, 'War's sorrow does not end when the guns cease firing', noting that on Remembrance Day we honour events that affected almost every Australian family:

> That earlier generation knew at first hand, as we cannot, all the horrors of the first great conflict of the 20th century, a conflict on an industrial scale, involving the mobilisation of 70 million soldiers

> around the world and resulting in the deaths of 13 million people, 9 million of them combatants. (*Age* 11 November 2008, p.10)

The *Australian*, writing of the more than 60 000 Australians who died between 1914 and 1918, concludes:

> We bear two obligations to those who died and the many thousands who lived on with awful injuries: never to forget what they did, and never to retreat from their still astounding example of generosity towards the defence of every people's liberty. (*Australian* 11 November 2008, p. 13)

On this day in 2008, the Governor-General of Australia leads a contingent of Australians dedicating a new memorial to the Australians who recaptured Le Hamel, on the Western Front. She then presides over a ceremony at the Australian War Memorial at Villers-Bretonneux with its thousands of soldiers' names and graves, where she is described as:

> ... doing what all visitors to this place do. Trying to connect with those lying there by reading the inscriptions, she was visibly moved, bending down and clearing foliage from a few of the graves. This place has a strong connection for all Australians. (*Age* 11 November 2008, p. 3)

The connection is also made on the village green in suburban Stirling, South Australia, where some 12 000 kilometres from the remembrance rituals in France, school children from the local primary school wear red poppies and stand quietly in the heat of the sun, to listen as the local member of parliament speaks of two men from the area whose lives were forever changed by their wartime experience. The small crowd is silent as a young girl reads John McCrae's poem, 'In Flanders Fields'. The bugler plays *Last Post*; wreaths are laid, and then children, teachers and the crowd drift away leaving the small plot of some 300 tiny white crosses, each

Figure 1 Stirling, South Australia, Remembrance Day 2008 (author's photo)

embellished with a red poppy as a sign to the passers-by of something far bigger than any one of them now might even imagine.

On 11 November in 1918, the members of the 27th Battalion AIF, a South Australian contingent which had served since early 1915, having pulled back from the fighting on the front line of the Somme battlefields to rest near Amiens after the final assault at Montebrehain, set out on a route march through several of the small villages. To the accompaniment of church bells and cheering villagers and with the battalion band playing the *Marseillaise*, they march to Berteaucourt. The Armistice has been signed. They had thought and planned for this day, anticipating wild celebrations. Yet their response was in the end one of 'mingled feelings': 'We were resting when the Armistice came and the troops did not get excited – just took it in their stride,' says one man (Woods 1980). The contrast with civilian reaction across the world is noted: ' ...thousands of civilians were carried away almost to the verge of insanity' (*BBD*[I], p. 197). For the remnants of a battle-weary battalion, 'Now the actual moment had arrived there was solemnity, born of grim memories' (*BBD*, p. 196).

Recalling that day and the 'blood lined' and 'hazardous trail that finally led to victory', the authors of the unit's history offered a poem by Arthur Noyes as an expression of their recollected feeling:

Peace? I recall an acre of the dead
Marks with the only sign on earth that saves:
The wings of death were hurrying overhead,
The loose earth shook on the on those unquiet graves

For the deep gunpits, with quick stabs of flame,
Made their own thunders of the sub-lit air;
Yet, as I read the crosses, name by names,
Rank after rank, it seemed that peace was there.

Sunlight and peace – a peace too deep for thought,
The peace of tides that underlie our strife,
The peace with which the moving heavens are fraught,
The peace that is our everlasting life.

The loose earth shook. The very hills were stirred.
The silence of the dead was all I heard. (*BBD*, p. 197)

Soon, the men of the battalion turn for home, meeting thereafter on ANZAC Day and Remembrance Day often marching in full uniform. On Remembrance Day 1933, they returned to the site of their beginnings as a fighting unit: the Mitcham Camp.

> RSL sub-Branch News
>
> Colonel Light Gardens
>
> Everything is in readiness for the 'Back-to-Mitcham Camp' celebrations to be held on Saturday (Armistice Day) ... No effort has been spared to make the celebrations one of the most novel reunions that has ever taken place. (*Advertiser* 8 November 1933)

****

By 1933, Mitcham Camp had ceased to exist except in memory. There were no recognisable landmarks. All that the men of the 27th Battalion had experienced in training there had been erased. In its place the splendid urban design experiment, the garden suburb of Colonel Light Gardens, had been established. On Remembrance Day, 150 men of the 27th Battalion CMF, many in their old uniforms, most in suits with hats as the fashion of the day demanded, marched behind the battalion band to Mortlock Recreation Park, on the south-western edge of the old Grange/Mortlock Park Estate. There, an aging Colonel Dollman, in a white tropical helmet, wearing his medals, and with bent body propped on a walking stick, took the salute. Dollman had been the first CO of the 27th and after his return from overseas service at the end of 1916, had been given command of the Mitcham Training Camp. There he remained until the end of the war. It was appropriate that he take the salute and provide as he did a written commentary for the day's festivities. He noted:

> Here it was that many thousands of the Australian Imperial Force were trained for that great adventure on which they embarked full of enthusiasm and national pride. Here they pledged their lives if need be for the good of their country, and learnt the art which enabled them to face their relentless foe with unconscious heroism and steadfastness. From here they marched to where the great grey ships waited to carry them to those final scenes of achievement victory, and too often, death ... I personally regret that when the town of Colonel Light Gardens was laid out on the historic site of the Mitcham Camp, no provision was made to perpetuate the importance and significance of the camp. (Colonel Walter Dollman 1933, in Miller 1986)

From this camp, thousands of men, including those of the 27th, the original unit and all reinforcements, left for service overseas and the battlefields of Gallipoli and the Western Front.[2] There, 1169 men of the 8000 who served with the 27th died and thousands more were wounded.

It is the intention here to trace the early days of the formation of the 27th Battalion as an exercise in constructing a biography of the unit that was known variously as Unley's Own and the Dinkums.[3] 'Places, like persons, have biographies ...', notes Tilley (1944, p. 33). People too build their lives on experience and then memory of spaces and places. The biographer of place or person has a particular responsibility to attempt to capture something of the place, the time and the intersection of people and spaces. As biographer Holmes says, 'The past does retain a physical presence for the biographer – in landscapes, buildings, photographs, and above all the actual trace of handwriting on original letters or journals' (1995, p. 67). Thus, he writes of the exercise and craft of biography as following in the footsteps, retracing the place and spaces:

> You would never catch them; no, you would never quite catch them. But maybe, if you were lucky, you might write about the pursuit of that fleeting figure in such a way as to bring it alive in the present. (Holmes 1995, p. 27)

He acknowledges, however, that spaces and places change:

> The material surfaces of life are continually breaking down, sloughing off, changing, almost as fast as human skin. A building is restored, a bridge is rebuilt or replaced, a road is widened or rerouted, a forest is cut down, a wooded hill is built over, a village green becomes a town centre. (Holmes 1995, p. 68)

It was just such change that Colonel Dollman regretted when he wrote a comment about Mitcham Camp, which for him and his men was in 1933 a 'landscape of memory' (Jordan 2008, p. 721) in the midst of a (by then, firmly established) suburb of the city of Adelaide, begun as it had been immediately after the war. Such evolution of the space erased collective memory of the four years that had forever changed the lives of the men who marched on the 300 acres of former farmland, wheat paddocks and scrub. Even though newspaper reports about the new purpose-designed garden suburb of 1924 noted:

> During its three or more years of martial activity thousands of South Australian soldiers were encamped upon it, and it was visited by thousands of relatives and friends of those almost forgotten warriors. For these reasons alone, it has a sentimental attraction for home buyers. (*Register* 31 January 1924, in Garnaut 1999, p. 68)

By 1925, perhaps even such sentimental attachment has disappeared for the new residents of Colonel Light Gardens:

> Adelaide has a new suburb ...Well-made macadamised roads, flourishing trees along the side walks, trim, well-kept gardens, and hordes of children have turned the paddock of a year ago into a modern suburb ... A butcher and grocer are carrying on business in premises especially set aside for such purposes ...There is a public garden at the north – west corner ... and already children play in it. Many of the occupied houses have their own little flower plots. (*Sunday Mail* 13 June 1925, in Garnaut 1999, p. 1)

While names having associations with the war period had been proposed (among them, Gallipoli and Cavell), Charles Reade, the town planner and promoter of the garden suburb concept, rejected such an inclination saying, ' ...nothing should be done to encourage any misconception as to the nature and purpose of the undertaking', the undertaking being a model garden suburb. Garnaut points out that his comments referred to ' ... names that had military connotations and might indicate that the suburb was exclusively for soldier settlement' (Garnaut 1999, p. 58). By 1933, the suburb was well established and had been named after Colonel William Light, who had laid out the City of Adelaide. Nothing remained of the Mitcham Camp, once the staging post for thousands of young men whose deeds are the stuff of history.

An exercise in retracing the men and places of the 27th Battalion as a biographical task is also an exploration of the spaces and places, of collective memory, of social memory, of urban memorials, and an exercise in what Karen Till has called geo-ethnography … an approach that focuses on why people make places to create meaning about how and where they are in the world, and how, in the process of place making, they communicate feelings of belonging and attachment. (Till 2005, p. 11).

Such an approach aligns with the tracing of urban landscapes and public memory work described by Hayden as: 'The power of place – the power of ordinary urban landscapes to nurture citizens' public memory, to encompass shared time in the form of shared territory …' (Hayden 1995, p. 9). Hayden's point in her work (which focuses on the lack of recognition of the urban history of ethnic communities and women's histories in American cities), is that such shared understanding of the meaning of the place ' … remains untapped for most working people's neighbourhoods …' (Hayden 1995, p. 9). As an urban historian, Hayden, like biographer Holmes, writes of the need to craft with imagination and to engage:

… social, historical, and aesthetic imagination to locate where narratives of cultural identity, embedded in the historic urban landscape, can be interpreted to project their largest and most enduring meanings for the city as a whole. (Hayden 1995, p. 13)

As a philosopher, Walter Benjamin worked into this process seeking to explore 'the debris of mass culture as the source of philosophical truth' (Buck-Morss 1991, p. ix). His hermeneutic strategy or 'dialectic of seeing' as process of using images, objects, 'fragments of historical data' suggests an interpretive process that can guide or inspire the present-day writer seeking the traces of the past in suburban landscapes. Buck-Morss, commenting on Benjamin's intention in the practice of history writing and his process in *Das Passagen-Werk* (The Arcades Project) writes:

His aim was to destroy the mythic immediacy of the present, not by inserting it into a cultural continuum that affirms the present as its continuum, but by discovering that constellation of historical

> origins which has the power to explode history's 'continuum'. In the era of industrial culture, consciousness exists in a mythic, dream state, against which historical knowledge is the only antidote. But the particular kind of historical knowledge that is needed to free the present from myth is not easily uncovered. Discarded and forgotten, it lies buried within surviving culture, remaining invisible precisely because it was of so little use to those in power. (p. x)

Nourishing the collective historical memory has implications for the possibility for action and change—simply put, we can learn from the past and if necessary contribute to the future.

Benjamin's method was to gather fragments and build a montage of impressions, ideas and images, while drawing on historical record and scholarly dissertations in philosophy, history, literature, political and social theory. Buck-Morss comments that he came to understood his trade not as an 'esoteric treatise writer' but as a 'mechanical engineer' (Buck-Morss 1991, p. 17). Adorno described Benjamin's method and thought as 'natural-historical', that is, 'The petrified, frozen, or obsolete inventory of cultural fragments spoke to him [...] as fossils or plants in the herbarium to the collector' (Adorno, in Buck-Morss, p. 58). This paper proceeds with an acknowledged respect for the ability to do this.

Thus, one can walk the streets of Colonel Light Gardens and allow some of the fragments of Mitcham Camp to speak. More than this, one can retrieve from the personal diary and letter fragments, from the newspapers of the times, and from family photos, and from the formal, published unit history, the way men of the 27th Battalion lived their lives at Mitcham Camp before embarkation for distance fields of battle. There are 'ghosts of historical things' (Nerval, quoted by Eiland & McLaughin, in Benjamin 1999, p. xii) in Colonel Light Gardens and 'times embedded in the spaces of things' (Eiland & McLaughlin, p. xi) in those suburban streets. Or, if we take Benjamin's line about the strolling attentions of the *flâneur*: 'The space winks at the *flâneur*:

What do you think may have gone on here?' (Benjamin 1982; trans Eiland & McLaughlin 1999, p. 419).

Benjamin asserted confidently that, 'in the course of *flânerie*, far-off times and places interpenetrate the landscape and the present moment' (p. 419). However, as Benjamin himself acknowledged, the days of the nineteenth-century *flâneur* had passed even as he describes the arcades of Paris in the 1920s and 30s. Buck-Morss makes the point that 'The utopian moment of *flânerie* was fleeting' (1999, p. 344).

The days of the *flâneur* who might stroll the streets of Colonel Light Gardens simply observing, taking in the scene, consuming the experience, would be well and truly gone in today's Australia. Yet, the possibilities of the digital technologies and, indeed, old-fashioned print publications allow us to create an ethnographic portrait: a montage, constructed from snippets and fragments which might tie people more firmly to the landscapes of the past in a quiet and leafy suburb. The purposeful present-day *flâneur* might thus take on a new domain for strolling, namely, the website and a digital repository of the past. This, however, is not the task here, although the accessibility of data and of image via the electronic media adds to the capacity of the researcher who not only walks the streets, but like Benjamin and others, spends hours in the library exploring archival materials to add to what Benjamin terms the 'colportage phenomenon of space' (Benjamin 1999, pp. 418–419).

Thus, the researcher as modern-day and purposeful and productive *flâneur*-cum-geo-ethnographer (Karen Till's term) or landscape archaeologist, as Christopher Tilley suggests, attempts to read the streets and spaces and describe them and thus reclaim them and represent them with empathy—this being a key attribute of Benjamin's *flâneur* but also of the ethnographer, as historian Greg Dening suggests:

> The art of ethnography is to see and then to narrate the socialities of that space, the gestures, the exchanges, the behavioural rules, the language, the silences. The art of ethnography is to catch all the things that dramatise experiences, in the broadest sense of the word dramatise – all those things that give the experience a beginning and an end – and emplot them. (Dening 1998, p. 153)

There are synergies with the biographer's craft here. Holmes argues that the biographer has a task comprising two elements: 'closely entwined strands'—the gathering of factual materials and then the relationship between the biographer and the subject. He talks of this as 'an imaginary' or 'fictional' relationship, 'a continuous living dialogue between the two as they move over the same historical ground, the same trail of events' (Holmes 1995, p. 66).

The historical ethnographer, as Mayne points out, also works with the 'mundane minutiae of documentary tracings ...' (Mayne 2000, p. 255), but also makes use of inter alia, photographs, plans, oral history, architectural studies, archaeology and archives research. It is, he says, the task of the historian to apply Bachelard's concept of 'the poetics of space' to the representation of the past. As Mayne explains, asserting the role of the ethnographies of place in historical work:

> Urban space is not a passive surface or neutral backdrop only contingently related to human activity. Any human site is necessarily invested with meanings simultaneously as the physical forms of its parts are made, reworked, and aggregated. (Mayne 2000)

This is territory understood, too, by Hayden as she describes the lives of ordinary folk in US cities, tracing landscapes, communities and individuals (Hayden 1995) There are synergies with the archaeologist of the landscape as Tilley suggests (1994) for he or she must be able to convey something of the intersections between the landscape and people:

> To understand a landscape truly it must be felt, but to convey some of this feeling to others it has to be talked about, recounted, or written and depicted. (1994, p. 31)

It seems obvious to state, as Holmes says, that the central purpose of 'the art and craft of biographical narrative (is) storytelling': … 'nonfiction storytelling' (Holmes 2008, p. 29). Further, ' … biography always takes the form of a human story, a narrative action, an agon' (2008, p. 29). Collective biography requires this of the writer as well. And, as Tilley asserts, 'Places, like persons, have biographies inasmuch as they are formed, used and transformed in relation to practice' (1994, p. 33). This requires attention to arts of narrative, and tellingly, he says, 'Places help to recall stories that are associated with them, and places only exist (as named locales) by virtue of their emplotment in narrative' (1994, p. 33) This says Tilley involves not description but 're-description' and a mimetic undertaking (p. 32).

This is what an ethnographic historian would do as does the *flâneur*. Mayne, as a historian, defines the process thus:

> Ethnographies of place, integrating history with geography and archaeology, enable rigorous interpretation of the hitherto inaccessible spheres of working-class households and neighbourhoods, revealing the complicated patterns and processes of local life in inner-city communities (Mayne 2000)

Thus it is also for the ethnographer of place. Or in the exercise here, where being the 'ethnographer of one's own situation'—walking the streets of a nearby suburb to build a connection with the past—is the 'way in' for calling up a time long gone. Capturing the past of Colonel Light Gardens and the Mitcham Camp and thus the 27th Battalion requires the writer who is seeking to 're-describe' and use imagination to see and depict what Greg Dening terms 'the fine-lined and faint webs of significance' about events, places and people, reflected in the artefacts of the past (Dening 1998, p. 208).

****

Goodwood Road extends from the city of Adelaide CBD, and leads to Colonel Light Gardens some five kilometres south. Traffic streams constantly past the commercial hoardings of car yards, homeware stores, the Goodwood Park pub, the art deco Capri Cinema (still operating and offering special performances of its theatre organ), motor repair shops, greengrocers, delicatessens, churches, school yards, a cycling shop, a florist, a butcher, supermarket, tax agent, accountant's office, medical centre, and so it goes—five kilometres of twenty-first-century trade mostly housed behind late nineteenth or early twentieth-century shop facades or ugly, minimalist, grey-walled, low-rise, cheaply constructed boxes of the 1960s and 70s.

One kilometre from the edge of the city, the road crosses Railway Terrace. Turn right here and one reaches Goodwood Railway Station. If you had travelled by train you would alight, double back along Railway Terrace, and stride three kilometres south to Doncaster Avenue. Here, you face the low rounded hills of the Mt Lofty Ranges and walk along the wide road leading to the planned centre of Colonel Light Gardens. At the time of the Mitcham Camp, this was the main driveway into what had been Grange Farm. Lined by huge river red gums, it seemed a fine entrance to a prosperous estate of crops, stock paddocks, and orchards of fruit and almond trees.

Imagine 200 metres further on and to your right, the original four-roomed, stone farmhouse: not grand but adequate when set aside as officers' quarters. Allow your eyes to scan the fields of hay, fruit trees and even vineyards and, in the distance, other houses tucked into the foothills. The gums still stand, although diminished in number, clearly marking a once impressive entry. The local council has hammered bird and possum boxes high on overhanging limbs. One has been commandeered by a swarm of bees. The farmhouse, now long gone, has been replaced by a rather unkempt house typical of the designs in the planned housing of the Garden City experiment of the 1920s. A rusting truck has been left to decay on what, in the 1930s, was almost certainly a manicured front garden.

Figure 2 Doncaster Avenue, Colonel Light Gardens, South Australia 2008. (author's photo)

Along this road, past this house and under the canopy of the tall gums, on Remembrance Day 1933, 150 members of the 27th Battalion AMF, having marched from Goodwood Crossing led by the battalion band to Mortlock Park, were inspected by Lieutenant Colonel Dollman.[4] The parade was held in conjunction with a 'Back to Mitcham' event. The day was not only one of commemoration, but also of furious activity, including athletics, shooting, riding contests, a motorcycle dispatch race, a machine gun competition, a camp-fire concert, a dance, a formal dinner, and in a marquee, a display of more than 300 photographs of the camp from its establishment on 1 April 1915 through to 1920. On display, photos of 169 units who had passed through the camp acknowledged the 50 000 young men who had marched, camped, exercised, and prepared for distant battlefields across the camp's 298 acres.[5]

BACK TO MITCHAM CAMP. SOLDIERS PLAY AT MORTLOCK PARK

> An outstanding feature was the war museum in a large marquee, which housed a remarkable collection of war trophies and souvenirs take from the enemy. "John Bradbury" 10/– note, issued in Egypt on the Bank of Constantinople, and overprinted in Arabic, was an exhibit of interest. The crosses of the 10th and 27th Battalions, which were erected in Pozieres in memory of those who fell in the fighting in July and August 1916, and the cross of the 50th Battalion erected to those who fell in the counter attack which retook Villers-Brettonneux in August 1918, were star exhibits.
> (*Advertiser* 13 November 1933, p. 11)

The immediate area of the Grange Farm and Mortlock Estate was the main campsite.[6] However, military orders gazetted that Mitcham Camp's boundaries extended several kilometres east, southeast, north and south. Today, people visiting Belair National Park or driving up Cross Road to Glen Osmond, or down south to the Flagstaff Hotel on the main South Road, would be surprised to think of soldiers on route marches, practising cavalry charges on horseback over bare paddocks, taking target practice, digging latrines and trenches or staging attacks and bayonet practice in the dusty valleys and plains over which they now travel on sleek highways through Adelaide's cream and red brick suburban landscape.

You might walk up Doncaster Avenue and emerge from the shaded path where you see ahead a pale, rose-coloured, stone cross and a large lump of sandstone set in a cleared area—a bare, treeless space unwatered and denuded of vegetation in this time of drought. Here the local RSL holds its ANZAC and Remembrance Day services.[7]

Perhaps no one thinks of the hub of the camp here, which then throbbed with army activities. Bell tents stretched as far as the horizon, huts surrounded the parade ground: huts for the hospital, a recreation hall, a post office, officers' quarters, reading rooms,

Figure 3 *Cross of Remembrance at the approximate site of the original parade ground, Mitcham Camp. (author's photo)*

church huts for six religious denominations, and a YMCA concert hall and bandstand.

Now stride south once more. Follow the route taken by the 27th as it marched to Mortlock Park. Today, the park is a location for recreational activities and remains a relatively lush green thanks to the use of bore water. At the north-eastern corner and close to the entrance of the Colonel Light Gardens Primary School, a triangle of gum trees stands in a small island of dry ground at the intersection of three streets. Look closely. Embedded in and gradually being swallowed by one of the trees are iron hoops for tethering horses.

The horses were watered at a pond at this spot and at the pond at Mortlock Park. These gums tell their story too. For here, photographers shuffled the men of each unit to order, under the trees,

Figure 4 *Recruits outside bell tents at Mitcham Camp, c. 1915. (author's photo)*[8]

with the soft outlines of the hills behind, faced them northwest so that the sun was behind the camera. They captured images of eager and, no doubt, anxious men before they marched away to entrain at Mitcham Railway Station for the journey to Outer Harbour and their transport overseas. The gums still stand; the men have gone.

Post-1918, the land, which had been purchased before the war by the state government specifically for the purpose of developing a garden suburb, was cleared and planning for the new suburb began. The first blocks north-east of what is now Colonel Light Gardens were offered in 1921. In 1924, the first of 400 homes under the new scheme was built. Miller notes that the area was intended 'partly for returned soldiers but not exclusively' (1986, n.p.) .Within ten years, even this intention seems to have been forgotten, for Colonel Dollman felt compelled to remind people of the suburb's origins.

When the 27th arrived in camp on 16 April 1915, they set about erecting tents on hard dusty ground. Shortly after, winter rains turned the

Figure 5 *Hoops embedded in the trees—a remnant from ninety years ago. (author's photo)*

camp on the ploughed and cleared fields into a quagmire of mud. Dust and mud were regular and expected conditions for all troops stationed there, even after the roads had been constructed and damped with tar. Gradually, an efficient working 'town' developed. The *BBD* claims that with the 'provision of hygienic and sanitary precautions', it was 'a model for the Commonwealth' (p. 14). There is a hint of the 'Boys' Own' adventure in the comment that:

> All ranks were accommodated in the old-fashioned and now discarded 'bell' tents, and set themselves with cheerfulness and thoroughness to make themselves as cosy as possible. (p. 14)

Men slept eight to a tent on the dirt floor. The winter of 1915 was particularly difficult; without huts or sheds (except for camp HQ) men existed and worked and trained in the wet in near-freezing temperatures. Latrines were pit trenches, shielded by flapping hessian sacking. Sickness and epidemics were frequent. One young

Figure 6 *Eleventh Reinforcements 27th Battalion Mitcham Camp, February 1916. Note the gums in the background. (photo courtesy of Chris Colyer)*

Figure 7 *The stand of gums still in position, 2009, with commemorative stone and plaque. (author's photo)*

soldier commented: 'The camp was more or less a bog hole. I was myself detailed to take part in at least two army burial parties' (Crase, in Miller 1986). Later recruits to the various units and to the 27th Battalion Reinforcements experienced the comfort of wood and iron huts and had access to all amenities. The Cheer Up Society and local businesses contributed resources and gifts to ease the troops' experience of life under canvass. Of particular note was a typewriter and a large clock, the latter presented by an old soldier. The clock was set up to ' ... record Regimental time on Gallipoli, and later in France' (*BBD*, p. 14).

Men spent up to six months in camp. These were days of routine and physical endurance. One young man described the experience:

> I had 2 blankets and one w.p. sheet.
>
> Reveille was sounded at 6 o'clock.
>
> Physical drill was carried out from 7 to 8 then breakfast —
> 9–12 drill 2–5 drill
>
> General leave within 1 mile of camp 5–9.30.
>
> So day after day this programme was carried on, with an occasional guard duty (all night) trench digging ...
>
> ... As we progressed in training the more difficult movements were commenced. For instance – for about a month prior to our embarkation we did a run of two or three miles every morning before breakfast finishing up with a stiff sprint over Hurdles etc
>
> (SSW notes for speech 1916)

Having marched in from Ascot Camp in April, the first contingent of the 27th departed for 'somewhere overseas' on 31 May 1915. They were to swap the relative comfort of Mitcham Camp for the unknown in Egypt, Gallipoli, England, France and Belgium. They had enlisted with enthusiasm, convinced that they were doing their duty for king and country, and to preserve the freedom and way of life they knew as Australians.

Before they embarked, the people of Adelaide acknowledged them with great fanfare. On 8 May, the *Advertiser* urged the public to celebrate and cheer the men.

Schoolchildren and teachers were pressed to line the streets as the battalion marched from the camp through Unley to the Jubilee Exhibition Building in Adelaide, to enjoy a luncheon prepared by the Cheer Up Society.

Pause today as you drive along Unley Road. Imagine the day when along Unley Road, with villas and cottages gradually giving way to neat shopfronts and the imposing façade of the Unley Town Hall, marched the original members of the 27th Battalion.

Lieutenant Colonel Dollman follows the band, leading the khaki-clad troops with slouch hats, puttees, polished boots and rifles shouldered. Flags wave, hats are thrust high, decorations of patriotic banners stream from the civic buildings. At the Unley Town Hall, there is a particularly fine display. Children lean out better to see the action; mothers beam with pride mingled with anxiety, and cheers cascade along the road as the battalion, in sharp formation, winds by. Here are young men thrusting forward to do their duty, galvanised by the exhortations of patriotism from worthy officials and the headlines in the daily press.

The first reports of 25 April 1915, where the ANZACs had gone into action at Gallipoli, were just reaching the local press. Reports from the Dardanelles had become the daily fare. The discourses of valour, honour, patriotism, courage, daring and sacrifice bombard the reader: 'New Siege of Troy', 'Australians in Action – Praised by the King', 'Worthy Sons of Empire' (*Advertiser* 15 May 1915, p. 15); 'Australians Win Imperishable Fame' (*Advertiser* 8 May 1915, p. 1).

Such were the headlines and reports soldiers and civilians alike read each day. Their eyes would have encountered headlines such as 'Storming the Dardanelles Heights', ' The Path of Duty is the Way to Glory', 'Thrilling Story of Superb Courage', 'Magnificent Cheerfulness of Dying Heroes' (*Advertiser* 8 May 1915).

The farewell parade and luncheon were captured enthusiastically in lengthy newspaper accounts and a multi-page pictorial supplement in the *Chronicle* (including a double-page photo of the men and officers of the 27th Battalion on the steps of the now-demolished Exhibition Building). Though described in only one cool paragraph in *BBD*, the event dominated Adelaide life for that day in May. After the grand parade, the Wondergraph advertised the picture show of the parade: 'Our Boys'—'This picture is really Magnificent' (*Advertiser* 12 June 1915). Excitement was high and the farewells numerous.

At one of the many official farewell events, Lieutenant Colonel Dollman responded to the good wishes expressed, as the unit history records, proclaiming that:

> The memorable landing on Gallipoli has been made, the first casualty lists have been published, and the men of the 27th fully recognized that the task before them is a 'dinkum soldier's' job. (*BBD*, p. 15)

On 12 May, members of the battalion once more gathered at the Unley Town Hall, where speeches by the governor and the mayor accompanied presentations of a pair of binoculars to Lieutenant Colonel Dollman and tokens to the local boys in the unit. Later the Governor reviewed the men on parade at Mitcham Camp and presented an Australian flag to the battalion. His words were typical of the patriotic rhetoric of the time:

> In bidding farewell to the men who are going away there is always pleasure and there is always a great deal of sadness in it. In this case with the pleasure and sadness is mingled with pride that we are

Figure 8 *The 27th Battalion outside the Jubilee Exhibition Building (since demolished) with insets of the march and luncheon celebration. (author's photo)*[9]

> adding to the splendid contingent already at the front men who will prove themselves equal. (Cheers) They are carrying with them not only the honor of Unley, the honor of their families and Australia, but they are carrying on their backs the honor of the British Empire. (Cheers)

He concluded the speech:

> ... we do not pity the men who have fallen. Their end was the finest in the world, and the end every soldier would wish to have. Our pity deep-hearted and respectful, goes out to those who are mourning the

> loss of the gallant dead … The price they have paid is a terrible price, but it is the price of Empire. (Cheers) (*Advertiser* 13 May 1915, p. 9)

Who then could imagine 2009 and a memorial park set opposite the town hall, the centrepiece of which is a gun captured by the 27th at one of the fierce battles of 8 August 1918.[10]

Who now, wiling away time in the quiet garden, remembers their story, the story of 'Unley's Own': the story of the boys who on 31 May 1915 marched from the relative comfort of Mitcham Camp to clamber aboard 'two special trains' for Outer Harbour?

Roused before dawn their excitement was palpable:

> So May 31st was The Day. At 4am the Bugles assembled for Reveille and when the first note sounded the whole battalion arose as one man and there went forth cheers – cheers full of expectancy – cheers of thankfulness that we were at last going to do our "Bit". I can nearly believe that every man kept awake all night so that he could send up such cheers. (Woods 1980)

Where today, luxury liners, gleaming blue and white, dock with tourists anxious to get ashore for the pleasures of wining and dining, shopping and the deliberate invasion of a new destination, the troopship, *Geelong*, dark, solid, and outfitted minimally for its purpose, gradually drew away from the cheering crowd. The regimental band played on the upper deck.

> And so they sailed, these men of the Twenty-Seventh Battalion, bound overseas to take their part in the mighty conflict between nations, leaving behind sorrowing but brave hearts to bear the suspense of separation, and to pray for the safe return of their dear ones. Slowly the troop ship leaves the wharf, the long streaming ribbons grow taut and snap, the band plays farewell music, to those on board the cheering grows faint, the groups of watching figures

> on the wharf merge into one another, and the homeland fades from sight (*BBD*, p. 16)

These were young men, aware of their role and the adventure of it all, yet scared and anxious:

> There was a great crowd to see us off. Mother and Dad, Ness and Cuth were all down on my behalf ... All were sad really, although all forced a smile. Couldn't look glum. Time enough for that after the ship left port ...
>
> At 4pm we pulled out and gradually the crowd on the wharf receded and shrank in size until we could not distinguish our own people. I found old Vick almost on the verge of tears in the stern soon after. (Telfer 1996, n.p.)

From Mitcham Camp, along the streets of the suburbs of Adelaide, they embarked for far-flung spaces; the 'Dinkums' became part of history.

On Remembrance Day and ANZAC Day, people gather to remember. These are specific occasions for memorialising. Yet in the suburbs, in a quiet corner, a small park, there are reminders—traces which bear witness to lives once lived there: 'There is no place that is not haunted by many different spirits hidden there in silence, spirits one can 'invoke' or not. (de Certeau, in Till 2005, p. 13).

The men who marched into and out of Mitcham Camp left more than material traces. For those who did not return, sepia photos stood on sideboards in almost every house in the city, suburbs and rural towns. For those who did, their children and grandchildren understood that something significant had happened, from words sometimes spoken—but more often not. There were traces, indelible and tacit, inscribed in family memories.

In an echo of de Certeau, Hauser says, 'Nothing that has happened or existed has left no trace, no material consequence' (2008, p. 189). There are traces, still, in Colonel Light Gardens of something of significance in the lives of many men and, thence, their descendents. Some of the men who knew the land as Mitcham Camp returned to purchase land in the new suburb—for this, after all, was what they had fought for, what they believed in as they endured long years away from home. Yet the suburb is just that, a suburb in a busy modern city. Hayden points out that:

> The places of everyday urban life are, by their very nature, mundane, ordinary, and constantly reused, and their social and political meanings are often not obvious. (Hayden 1995, p. 49)

She goes on to suggest, 'It takes a great deal of research, community involvement, and inventive signing and mapping to bring these meanings out, ...'. The outcome might then be 'a shared process leading to shared public meanings' (1995, p. 49).[11]

Colonel Dollman wanted the space of Mitcham Camp to be remembered, for he knew its imperative for the men who trained there. The brass plaque that describes the iron holds for tethering horses tells nothing of the stories of these men—the individual and collective biographies of the 27th Battalion and others. This place has memories—stories that connect the past of this landscape to the present. How such stories can be told and how the suburban streetscape can be enlisted in the telling of the past is the challenge to be met, so that collective and social memories depend not only on ritual occasions but also on a daily interaction with the past. Connecting the biography of the landscape to the biographies of men and the collective biography of the 27th Battalion is a task to be continued.

Notes

1. *The Blue and Brown Diamond at War* is the unit history of the 27thBattalion, AIF. The authors, Lieutenant Colonel W Dollman, and Sergeant H Skinner worked with a publications committee, all members of the battalion, to write and publish the history in 1921. Hereafter whenever the book is quoted it is referenced as *BBD* to indicate the historical source of the material.
2. Miller suggests that between 30 000 and 50 000 men passed through the camp. Col Dollman, in a commemorative booklet published for the 'Back to Mitcham Camp' celebration in 1933, repeated figures from his 1918 final report to District Military Headquarters: 'During the continuance of the Camps, the total of enlistments in the 4th Military District was 36,000' (in Colyer 2003).
3. Lieutenant Colonel Dollman, the first CO of the 27th, speaking at a function in early 1915 saying, 'that the task before them is a "dinkum soldier's job"'. This term stuck and spread through to the whole Australian army. Dollman was the mayor of the suburb of Unley, which adjoined the area of the Mitcham Camp. 'It is little surprise that the 27th, as well as being "Unley's Own", became "Dollman's Dinkum Diggers," and more familiarly, "Dolly's Dinkum Diggers"' (Colyer 2003).
4. Dollman was a lieutenant-colonel during the war, but was promoted to the rank of colonel after he retired.
5. The numbers are variously given as between 30 000 and 50 000 (Miller 1986).
6. 'The tented and training area more generally known as Mitcham Camp was bounded by Goodwood Road, Grange Road, View Street, Winnall Street, and Springbank Road as they are now known' (Miller 1986).
7. The reserve was set aside during the development of the new suburb 'To preserve its association with the historic Mitcham Camp ... on the site of the old Camp Headquarters. This has been planted with evergreen shrubs and an arch had been erected as memorial' (*Advertiser* 7 August 1937, in Miller 1986). Perhaps Colonel Dollman's lament in 1933 had some influence.
8. From a contemporary photo originally in the *Observer* newspaper, Adelaide (Dollman papers, courtesy of Chris Colyer).
9. From contemporary photos in *For King and Empire*, a special supplement in the *Chronicle* newpaper, Adelaide, 29 January 1916, pp. 12–13.
10. The captured gun was dedicated on 31 July 1920 with Colonel Dollman officiating at the ceremony in Unley. *The Blue and Brown Diamond* records the capture on 8 August 1918 at Villers-Bretonneux: 'Chief amongst the 27th Battalion captures were: - 9 77-mm guns, 1 plant, 25 machine guns, 2 officers and 200 other ranks prisoners' (*BBD*, p. 154).

11. The Mitcham Historical Society/CLHS are mindful of their role in this and have a website devoted to photos of Mitcham Camp. There is room, however, to expand this with documents and data that might speak of the men who passed across its vast spaces.

References

Ackroyd, P 2003, *London: The Biography*, Anchor Books, London.

Benjamin, W 1999, *The Arcades Project*, trans H Eiland & H McLaughlin, based on the German volume edited by Rolf Tiedemann, Harvard University Press, Cambridge, Massachusetts.

Best, N 2008, *The Greatest Day in History – How The Great War Really Ended*, Phoenix/Orion Books, London.

Buck-Morss, S 1991, *The Dialectics of Seeing – Walter Benjamin and the Arcades Project*, MIT Press, Cambridge, Massachusetts.

Colyer, C 2003, *Dolly's Dinkum Diggers*, unpublished MS, prepared for the exhibition of the same name, City of Unley, 2003.

Dening, G 1998, *Readings/Writings*, Melbourne University Press, Carlton South, Victoria.

Dollman, W & Skinner, HM 1921, *The Blue and Brown Diamond at War*, Lonnen & Cope, Adelaide.

Garnaut, C 1999, *Colonel Light Gardens – model garden suburb*, Crossing Press, Darlinghurst, NSW.

Hayden, D 1995, *The Power of Place – Urban Landscapes as Public History*, MIT Press, Cambridge, Massachusetts.

Holmes, R 1995, *Footsteps – Adventures of a Romantic Biographer*, Hammersmith, Flamingo, London.

Holmes, R 2008, 'Biography: The Past has a Great Future', *Australian Book Review*, no. 306, November.

Hauser, K 2008, *Bloody Old Britain – O.G.S.Crawford and the archaeology of Modern Life*, Granta Books, London.

Jordan, J 2008, 'Violence, Memory and Politics: Recent Work on Memorials in Berlin and Beyond', review essay, *Journal of Urban History*, viewed 29 Sept 2008, pp. 718–724, <http://juh.sagepub.com>.

Mayne, A 2000, 'On the Edge of History', *Journal of Urban History*, vol. 26, p. 249–256, viewed 29 Sept 2008, <http://juh.sagepub.com>.

Miller, RJ 1986, *50 000 Men : A Short History of Mitcham Camp and of the men who trained there 1915-1918*, commemorative booklet, Mitcham Camp Memorial 23 March 1986, Colonel Light Gardens,.

Telfer, R, 1996, DAD'S WAR DIARIES, ed C Taplin, (self-published).

Till, K 2005, *The New Berlin – Memory, Politics, Place*, University of Minnesota Press, Minneapolis.

Tilley, C 1994, *A Phenomenology of landscape: places, paths, monuments*, Berg Publishers, Oxford.

Woods, SS 1980, unpublished MS, personal collection of the author.

Chapter 7

Counting on archives

William Park and John Cokley
University of Queensland

Remnants of war history exist in our minds, in our media and in our communal records, and this chapter focuses on the link between those areas: the trust we as individuals afford to the records. People trust records they can show to be true and they do not trust records which they can show to have even one mistake; you do not know whether the single mistake is the only one, or one of many. Our recent research—as William Park undertook his Master of Philosophy dissertation on the Australian *World War 2 Nominal Roll*—has shown that much of this communal record of Australians at war is incomplete and flawed (Park 2009). That immediately affects the media remnants, because reporters and editors routinely refer to archival 'communal' memory for anniversary stories about the commencement of war, the cessation of hostilities and major battles, events and hero stories along the way. And these media remnants directly affect those in our minds and in the minds of our children. It is a cyclical and repeating process.

Having discovered this flawed nature of the central database of records, we now propose in a wider arena the methodology which we think will mitigate the problem. Appropriately, the methodology is a product of Bill Park's personal as well as professional experiences and offers an insight into one way of viewing and dealing with these particular remnants of war: the primary sources.

Background

Bill Park: I came to the role of 'researcher of war archives' as an accountant. When I graduated from the Church of England Grammar School in Brisbane in 1938 I enrolled in a certificate of accounting and a part-time commerce degree at the University of Queensland in 1939. I originally wanted to become an engineer but the careers adviser at school told me to look for 'anything to do with figures' and I ended up in accounting. And 'anything to do with figures' has become the story of my life. During my commerce studies, I was called up for compulsory military training in the Australian army and found myself in the 15th Battalion, headed for New Guinea. In short order, the Japanese started the Pacific War and I spent the duration in the army. But not just any part of the army: my head for figures landed me in the Intelligence and Signals Corps, coding and decoding all army messages sent by wireless. Right there I learnt how important accuracy was because even one mistake could cost us lives and could even lose the war. This was reinforced by the rule that mistakes would land us on a charge, resulting in punishment and an entry on our military record. Back on 'Civvie Street' after the war, I continued my studies and graduated in 1947 with a Bachelor of Commerce, which launched me on my business career. I discovered that the key element of studying commerce, and working as an accountant, is the principle of double-entry bookkeeping. We learnt about the fifteenth-century mathematician Frater Luca Bartolomes Pacioli (and his friend Leonardo da Vinci) who promoted the double-entry method, and a thirteenth-century Florentine banker's account book, the earliest known evidence of the double-entry system.[1]

John Cokley: I came to this role as a journalist who spent more time in the newspaper library and archives—when they existed physically rather than merely virtually—than many of my colleagues, because I felt drawn to ferret out that 'last little detail', which I hoped would turn otherwise ordinary stories into really special stories, and even the special stories into things which readers would talk about for a long time after they had finished with the day's news. During my earliest years in newspapers, libraries contained 'real books'—paper printed then bound with cloth and card—and our company archives were bursting with clippings from old newspapers and magazines, laboriously identified, labeled and filed by dedicated librarians who knew exactly how to find what journalists needed, even under the crazy pressures of production deadlines. I learned from these colleagues that there was always one more file you could check, one more biography on the shelf, and one more clipping stuck to the back of the pile which would probably have the nugget of information I needed.

Detail and accuracy should be important to all journalists but there is one genre which uses such files more than any other: anniversary journalism, where reporters and editors pull together stories and facts from important past events to produce special supplements or editions. In the latter half of the twentieth century and even today, special editions (in print, broadcast and online) have been produced remembering the big moments of World War 2, even World War 1, and other world-changing events such as the death of US President John F Kennedy, the disappearance of Australian Prime Minister Harold Holt, the first moon landing in 1969, the Challenger space shuttle disaster in 1986, and the deaths of Diana, Princess of Wales and Mother Teresa in 1997. Since then, there has been a glut: the September 11 attacks in 2001, the invasion of Iraq in 2003, and the election of the United States' first black president in 2008. If these special editions are going to be factual and trustworthy, not cluttered with errors, then the archives themselves have to be factual and error free, at least as far as possible. Perhaps it was my long association with pedantic and careful newspaper librarians, but I never dreamed that this would not be the case, until I met Bill Park in 2006.

Twelve years earlier, 1994 was especially prominent, being the fiftieth anniversary of D-Day. There was intense public, media and institutional interest in the feats and casualties of the Normandy invasion of June 1944. Many newspaper and television invasion anniversary supplements were published and became collectable souvenirs. More followed the next year to mark the anniversary of the end of the war in Europe and the Pacific theatres. The seventieth anniversary of the start of hostilities will likely produce another crop of supplements. Both Bill and I had a personal interest in the 1994 publications: Bill, as a veteran of World War 2 active service, and me, as the son of another veteran, Keith Cokley, also in Bill's unit, Australia's 15th Battalion. As a subeditor on the News Corporation's weekly newspaper, the *Sunday Mail,* I worked on a rolling stream of anniversary supplements.

The idea of the Australian government creating its own 'anniversary supplement', an online memorial to WW2 service men and women, emerged in 1996 with the compilation of the *Vietnam Nominal Roll* (Source X[2] 2009, personal communication). The Department of Defence called for a single database containing the names of those who had served in the Vietnam conflict (1963–1972), and the first *Vietnam Nominal Roll* was produced in printed book form. A number of letters and complaints followed, highlighting errors and omissions; so much so, that a second edition, incorporating the necessary amendments, was produced in 1997, but this time also on CD. The *Korean Nominal Roll* was produced in book form in 1998, after which the rolls were digitised and uploaded to Internet websites. Such celebration of wartime anniversaries, including ANZAC Day, became almost a national pastime (*cf* Mackay 2008, p. 11), led by the newly-elected conservative prime minister, John Howard. There arose a movement to collect and publish on the Internet, in the form of the *World War 2 Nominal Roll (WW2NR)*,[3] the names of all WW2 dead, and later the names of all those who served in the war. The Returned and Services League of Australia (RSL) suggested that similar nominal rolls be produced for all wars in which the Commonwealth had been involved since Federation, particularly World Wars 1 and 2; the rolls were to be ready in time for the Centenary of Federation in 2001, and funded by money set aside for the celebrations (Source X 2009, personal communication). The RSL's suggestion was approved and work started in 1998–99.

****

The *WW2NR* (derived from its web address) became a 'virtual' war memorial because the data it contained both represented and physically reflected data and objects stored in the Australian War Memorial (AWM) buildings in Canberra, as the digital data was served to the Internet community as a series of text and image files using web browsers. But its limitations became evident almost immediately. In 2003, as part of family and veterans' gatherings and recollections, Bill Park obtained a copy of a seventeenth-century muster roll (*cf* Gibson & Dell 1989) for the Scottish army in Scotland. He thought, not unreasonably, that if he could obtain an army muster roll from seventeenth-century Scotland, he could obtain a muster roll from twentieth-century Australia. Specifically, he wanted to obtain, from the University of Queensland, a list of his mates who had been called up with him, in 1941, for training with a militia infantry battalion before the start of hostilities with Japan, and who had then been transferred to full-time duty with that unit and had gone off to war.

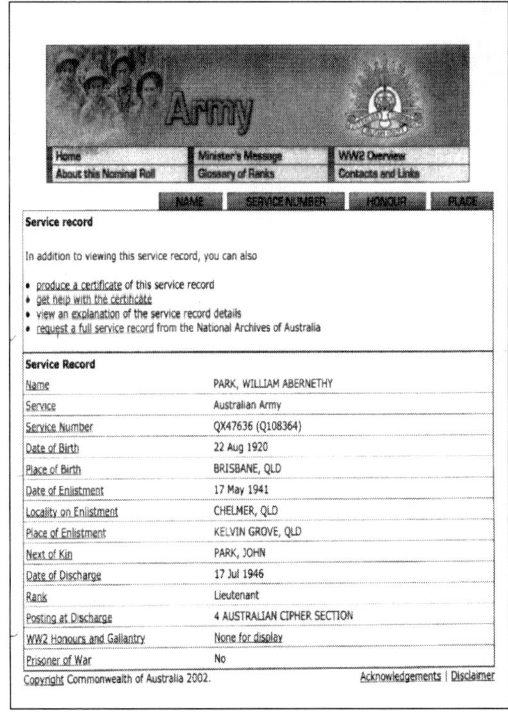

Army

Home	Minister's Message	WW2 Overview
About this Nominal Roll	Glossary of Ranks	Contacts and Links

NAME | SERVICE NUMBER | HONOUR | PLACE

Service record

In addition to viewing this service record, you can also

- produce a certificate of this service record
- get help with the certificate
- view an explanation of the service record details
- request a full service record from the National Archives of Australia

Service Record	
Name	PARK, WILLIAM ABERNETHY
Service	Australian Army
Service Number	QX47636 (Q108364)
Date of Birth	22 Aug 1920
Place of Birth	BRISBANE, QLD
Date of Enlistment	17 May 1941
Locality on Enlistment	CHELMER, QLD
Place of Enlistment	KELVIN GROVE, QLD
Next of Kin	PARK, JOHN
Date of Discharge	17 Jul 1946
Rank	Lieutenant
Posting at Discharge	4 AUSTRALIAN CIPHER SECTION
WW2 Honours and Gallantry	None for display
Prisoner of War	No

Copyright Commonwealth of Australia 2002. Acknowledgements | Disclaimer

Figure 1 Bill Park's service record, obtained from the WW2NR

This was not to be the case. Although the *WW2NR* had been published the previous year, and although his own service record appeared online, his searches suggested that many of the individuals he clearly recalled being involved were either omitted from the roll or listed incorrectly. He called on his contacts at the University of Queensland and was directed to the university's archives in the Parnell Building. But stored lists of enrolments, graduations, enlistments and commemorations of service, even on the publicly displayed University Roll of Honour, failed to give a unified and complete record. Bill became determined to compile his own list and, along the way, put right what he had concluded was a set of historical inaccuracies. Checkpoints on this journey included the archives of the University of Queensland, the Office of Australian War Graves, the AWM, and the National Archives of Australia. However, no single source proved to be sufficient, and each one required a high degree of background knowledge about the stored data, knowledge which we came to identify as *context*. Simply knowing the facts about an individual soldier's service record was not enough; the researcher had to know *about* the facts and their historical and cultural context. It also helped, and turned out to be essential, to know the story of the soldier, drawn from personal testimony. So, before proceeding to the facts discovered, we should discuss the context of this data, how this emerged for us, and how this fits into the process of double-entry book-keeping as applied to the *WW2NR*.

The context of a memorial: testimony

War memorials often represent a process of negotiation and have a plurality of meanings (Hope 2003, p. 94). A memorial, whether a simple monument or a museum, contains within it not only a superficial gesture towards remembrance and the dead but a wealth of information about the priorities, politics and sensibilities of those who built it. The purpose of a memorial is as much to resolve traumatic memories as to preserve them. For both individuals and for societies affected by death in war, commemoration needs to achieve a degree of closure and resolution of suffering as part of the mourning process, through 'the creation of an appropriate memory' (Whitmarsh 2001, p. 10). It requires testimony and testimony seems to come hard to Australians.

Our country in 1900 was almost bare of testimony to the wars for territory between Aborigines and the English arrivals in the eighteenth century. Aborigines had raised no legible monuments to either their own traditional civil wars or their resistance against the invaders, and the newcomers seldom commemorated conflicts between black and white (Inglis 2005, p. 21). But after the Boer War (1899–1902), memorials began to change the landscape. Some 500 soldiers out of 15 000 who served in South Africa died in action or of wounds or disease. Initially, as the news came through, many of them were accorded individual tablets or honour boards in town halls, churches or schools. Sometimes, outdoor monuments, more visible than tablets on walls, were erected. However, as further bad news came through, local committees were set up to raise funds for combined memorials in local areas (Inglis). The Heraldry and Genealogy Society of Canberra website (2009) notes that there are still about 100 or so Boer War memorials in existence.

On about seventy-five per cent of the Boer War memorials raised in Australia, only the dead are named, usually in order of rank. It is remarkable, however, that on the other twenty-five per cent the names of the living are recorded as well; this practice departs from a British military tradition which gives individual honour on monuments only to the dead. More commonly than anywhere else, Australia listed on more than half its World War I memorials the names of the men who had returned as well as those who had died (Inglis 2005, pp. 182–184). This practice is virtually unknown in France and Italy, rare in the US, and quite uncommon in the UK, Canada and New Zealand. Perhaps this was because the Australian colonies had only tiny regular forces and their contingents were formed almost entirely of part-time soldiers volunteering to serve overseas. Fellow citizens, in some places, decided that such volunteering should be recognised and that volunteers' names be recorded on each monument. Nobody expected federal, state or municipal governments to pay for the memorials; it was understood this was a communal rather than an official responsibility (Inglis 2005, pp. 44–50) and local committees determined whose names would appear on the memorials.

While some of the inscriptions on early monuments began and ended with simple facts of history, it was not long before most inscriptions moved from history to tribute and testimony. Those named on the memorial are saluted as boys, sons, lads, comrades, citizens, soldiers, men. The voluntary character of the AIF is affirmed in a variety of phrases with that special Australian resonance deriving from the absence of conscription. The soldiers fought *for*, not *against*. They fought for freedom and liberty, for victory, for justice, for the right and the good (Inglis 2005). More than 6000 war memorials erected by citizens around Australia become focal points for ANZAC Day and similar commemorations. Federal tax deductions were allowed for the building of 'war memorials' in the form of swimming pools, sports ovals, public buildings and some churches (Inglis 2005, p. 352).

Testimony and memory

Memory has been the major preoccupation for social thinkers since the Greeks (Olick & Robbins 1998, p. 106) and the construction and narration of a memory, such as in contemporary journalistic practice, derives from the oral and epic traditions of storytelling, the same traditions that gave birth to the chronicle and then to history (Thelen 1989, p. 1118). While memory is private and individual, it is also collective and cultural and is constructed, not merely reproduced; this construction is not made in isolation but in dialogue with others in the contexts of community, broader politics, and social dynamics (Thelen 1989, p. 1119). Thus, the socially constructed nature of memory suggests that the accuracy of a memory, with how it correctly describes what actually occurred at some point in the past, is essential to authentic construction and reconstruction. Individuals compare different accounts of the same event and evaluate which is most accurate (Thelen 1989, p. 1119).

Collective memory is also home to critical aspects of political culture, community tradition and social identity. Communication makes possible the unique capacity of collective memory to preserve pasts older than the oldest living individual and the media (including journalism) are extremely important to the construction and maintenance of a national collective memory (Edy 1999, p. 72). Stories told and retold by reporters affect how individuals see themselves as one community or many groups (p. 73).

Stories about the past appear regularly in the news in three basic forms: commemorative (sometimes called anniversary journalism) that does not attempt to connect the past to the present in meaningful ways, historical analogies that attempt to make the past relevant to the present by using a past event as a tool to analyse and predict the outcome of a current situation, and historical contexts that trace the portions of the past that appear relevant in leading up to the present circumstances (Edy 1999, pp. 74–80). This reinforces the view that the accuracy of the storage mechanisms—both journalistic archives and the national kind—is essential to the discussion of collective memory.

The range of errors which affects journalists' credibility depends on the point of view of the observer (Meyer 2004, pp. 83–108). In a two-year study of US newspapers, at least one objective (hard) error—spellings, addresses, titles, dates etc—was identified in twenty-one per cent of all stories sampled. At least one subjective (soft) error—quotes out of context, interviews distorted etc—was identified in fifty-three per cent of all stories. At least one maths error—numbers wrong, misleading or misinterpreted—was identified in eighteen per cent of all stories. Overall, Meyer suggests that fifty-nine per cent of all stories sampled had at least one error. He suggests that perception of any kind of error undermines credibility (p. 84) but the subjective error category is the most damaging. Minor maths errors can cause as much distrust as major soft errors. Maths errors are not ambiguous and it only takes a small one to trigger mistrust. Subjective errors are ambiguous and sources recognise this and discount them to some extent—but not enough to keep them from being an important source of lost credibility (p. 96).

The top reason given by sources (Meyer 2004, p. 102) when asked to judge why the reporter made a mistake was simply that the reporter did not understand what he or she was writing about. A newspaper that is understaffed will be more susceptible than one that is not. Meyer also suggests that the competence of reporters and copyeditors makes a difference in the error rate observed, and that journalists need a working knowledge of the subjects they cover and programs for lifelong learning to improve accuracy rates.

Is the *WW2NR* trustworthy? Bill's exhaustive study over the past few years confirms that it is only slightly more factually reliable than the newspapers mentioned above: among Australians who served in the militia, 10.31 per cent of their militia service is missing from the roll. At least fifty-one per cent of entries surveyed were inaccurate and forty-six per cent of individuals are listed with an incorrect or missing AIF enlistment date.

Whatever its developers intended, the nominal roll has become much more than just an archive of facts. It fulfills many of the roles completed by journalists—discovering, establishing, editing, contextualising, recording and publishing memory, including the ability to update and, where necessary, correct. But the record shows that the contractor hired for the job tendered on the basis of demonstrated skills in records management, and an objective methodology which promised quality assurance, not on the basis of context or testimony, and in our discovery of many factual errors, it is those things—context and testimony—which have been shown to be most lacking. And so we come to our application of 'double-entry bookkeeping' to the *WW2NR*.

The story of the roll

When establishing the nominal roll, Veterans' Affairs decided to engage a contractor to do the work due to the estimated one million people and at least that number of files involved (*WW2NR* website 2002). The quality assurance process is published on the same website, detailing 'a four-check process ... (using) a double-entry computer process'.

> Each record had its information entered by one operator and then entered again by a different operator. The computer program compared the two entries and identified any differences between the two. If a discrepancy appeared the computer program required the second operator to re-examine the service document before the record could be processed further. This method was designed to eliminate typographical and data source errors normally encountered in a highly intensive data entry environment.

The *WW2NR* website methodology also identified a production supervisor 'sign-off check' in which

> individual records would be grouped and sorted so that similar information could be compared and obvious errors or omissions rectified before the work was signed off from the production line.

That sign-off comprised 'a final internal review by the contractor's production manager ... conducted prior to each fortnightly external audit'. The website noted that 'thousands of records were reviewed to correct any major errors' (*WW2NR* website 2002). The contractor was paid based on an agreed minimum daily output (Source X 2009, personal communication).

This methodology explicitly includes the term 'double-entry', but what it implicitly excludes is that other 'double-entry' method we have discussed, emphasising context and testimony. Bill's massive research project (Park 2009) clearly suggests that the mechanistic double-entry handling of the datasheets provided to the contractor in the early part of this century was insufficient to eliminate a vast array of errors. The only way these errors have been discovered—not only by Bill but by the many other ordinary Australians, both veterans and their descendents, who have complained to Veterans' Affairs—is by the two-fold application of context and testimony: personal or primary source knowledge of how and when soldiers enlisted, what happened when they did, how their ordinary lives proceeded in the army, how they were paid, and how they were eventually discharged and returned to civilian life. Let's see what happens in that kind of double-entry historical book-keeping.

Army records

The *WW2NR* memorandum makes it clear that the source records used for information about Australian army service were the Oath of Enlistment (Attestation), the record of service and discharge forms. Those forms were filed by the army in the army service records—separate files for each soldier, which contained those forms and any other relevant information about the soldier's service. Pay and allowances records were kept by the army accounts or finance offices. For most WW2 army personnel, the individual service records are now held by the National Archives Office in Canberra, but the individual pay records for Queensland soldiers are held by the National Archives Office in Brisbane.

The service record is the army's file on each individual soldier—a personnel file. In it are such papers as the Oath of Enlistment (Attestation) Form(s); Service and Casualty Forms (on which are recorded in detail allocation/transfers to units, promotions, casualties, illnesses, embarkation etc), discharge papers and other papers relating to the specific person. The army service record does not contain the pay records, which were maintained and kept separately.

All available army service records for WW2 soldiers (other than those who later enlisted in the postwar army) are now located at the National Archives Offices in Canberra. They can be accessed by personal visit. Photocopies are made available on request and on payment of a fee for each file. Some files have been digitised and are available on the archives website.[4] The three papers in the army service record that are of interest for the *WW2NR* are described below.

Oath of Enlistment (Attestation) Form

This is a form that was signed by an army recruit on enlistment. There were a number of different forms, because there were a number of different 'armies' in the Australian army just prior to, and during, WW2. Also, sometimes even the form for the same 'army' had to be altered from time to time. So there is no such thing as one standard attestation form. However, they all have at least one thing in common—the Oath of Enlistment signed by every recruit. The soldier's file should contain all the attestation forms he signed during his military career—for example, the (militia) Attestation Form when he enlisted in the Citizen Military Forces (CMF) and an (AIF) Attestation Form if he re-enlisted in the AIF. The Attestation Form is very important for entry on the *WW2NR*. It gives the information for name, service number, date and place of birth, date and locality on enlistment (the date and place when and where the Oath of Enlistment was signed), and next of kin. Most importantly, it tells precisely what the recruit signed by way of his oath to serve. It is the key to correct entry of most of the information shown on the *WW2NR*. Some, but not all, of that information may be in other records.

A copy of Bill Park's attestation form for compulsory military training and the militia and his attestation form for the AIF are included here. The first form was partly completed (but not signed) when Bill was called up for a medical examination in April 1940. It was resurrected in May 1941, when he passed another medical examination and signed the form on 17 May. That date is regarded as his official enlistment date although he did not actually go into camp until November 1941. That signed form enabled the army to call up the recruit for ninety

MILITIA

A.A. Form Mob. 1

AUSTRALIAN  MILITARY FORCES

MOBILIZATION ATTESTATION FORM

To be filled in for all Persons at the Place of Assembly when called out under Parts III. or IV. of the Defence Act, or when voluntarily enlisted.

Army No. Q108364

Surname PARK. (BLOCK CAPITALS) *Christian Name* William Abernethy.

Unit 15 Bn (Arr Camp)

Enlisted for war service at KELVIN GROVE, BRISBANE. (Place)

Queensland (State) 21 NOV 1941 (Date)

TERMINATION
APPOINTMENT
17-7-46

A

*Questions to be put to persons called out or presenting themselves for voluntary enlistment.**

1. What is your name?	1. Surname PARK (BLOCK LETTERS) Other names William Abernethy.
2. Where were you born?	2. In or near the town of Brisbane in the state or country of Queensland
3. Are you a British Subject?	3. N.B.B.S.
4. What is your age and date of birth?	4. Age 19 years 7 months. Date of Birth 22 : 8 : 1920.
5. What is your trade or occupation?	5. Clerk
6. Are you married, single or widower?	6. Single
7. Have you previously served on ~~active service~~? If so, where and in what arm?	7. NO.
8. Who is your actual next of kin? (Order of relationship:—wife, eldest son, eldest daughter, father, mother, eldest brother, eldest sister, eldest half-brother, eldest half-sister)	8. Name John Rutherford Park Address "Tresta" Laurel Ave Chelmer Relationship Father
9. What is your permanent address?	9. "Tresta" Laurel Avenue Chelmer
10. What is your religious denomination? (This question need not be answered if the man has a conscientious objection to doing so)	10. C of E

I, William Abernethy Park do solemnly declare that the above answers made by me to the above questions are true.

Witnessed by [illegible] (*Signature of Attesting or Witnessing Officer*) Park *Signature*

*The person will be warned that should he give false answers to any of these questions he will be liable to heavy penalties under the Defence Act.

Figure 2 *The (militia) Attestation Form Bill Park signed when he enlisted in the Citizen Military Forces. (National Archives)*

B

MEDICAL EXAMINATION

I have made full and careful examination of the abovenamed person in accordance with the instructions contained in the Standing Orders for Australian Army Medical Services. In my opinion he is—*

1. Fit for Class I.
2. ~~Temporarily unfit for Class I.~~†
3. ~~Fit for Class II.~~
4. ~~Temporarily unfit for Class II.~~†
5. ~~Unfit for military service~~†

Place KELVIN GROVE, BRISBANE Date 6: 4: 1940.

Signature of Examining Medical Officer C. McCarthy

*Classifications which are inapplicable to be struck out. † Reasons for unfitness to be stated.

C

OATH OF ENLISTMENT‡

For persons voluntarily enlisted or called upon under Part III. or Part IV. of the Defence Act to serve in the Citizen Forces in time of war. Not compulsory for serving members of the Forces or those allotted to the Citizen Forces under Part XII. of the Act, but unless in any case an objection is raised, the oath should be administered to them as part of the ceremony of attestation.

I, William Abernethy Park swear that I will well and truly serve our Sovereign Lord, the King, in the Military Forces of the Commonwealth of Australia until the cessation of the present time of war or until sooner lawfully discharged, dismissed, or removed, and that I will resist His Majesty's enemies and cause His Majesty's peace to be kept and maintained, and that I will in all matters appertaining to my service faithfully discharge my duty according to law.

So help Me God!

Signature of Person Enlisted Park

Subscribed at KELVIN GROVE, BRISBANE in the State of Queensland

this 17 day of May 1941

Before me—

Signature of Attesting Officer

‡Persons who object to take an oath may make an affirmation in accordance with the Third Schedule of the Defence Act. In such case the above form will be amended accordingly and initialed by the Attesting Officer.

TERMINATION
APPOINTMENT

APPROVED
RECRUITING MAN POWER OFFICER
17 MAY 1941

Figure 3 The (militia) Attestation Form Bill Park signed when he enlisted in the Citizen Military Forces (back). (National Archives)

days training (which it did by written notice in November 1941) and also in February 1942 to call him up for full-time duty for the duration of the war without any further enlistment forms being signed.

The second form was completed when Bill volunteered to 'transfer' to the AIF. Technically, he was discharged from the CMF and enlisted in the AIF on 6 February 1943.

AUSTRALIAN MILITARY FORCES.

A.A. Form A.200. (Revised April, 1941.)

ATTESTATION FORM.

FOR SPECIAL FORCES RAISED FOR SERVICE IN AUSTRALIA OR ABROAD.

Army No. QX47636

Surname PARK (BLOCK CAPITALS) Other Names William Abernethy

Unit

Enlisted for service at Brisbane (Place)

Q'sland (State) 4/2/43 (Date)

A. *Questions to be put to persons called out or presenting themselves for voluntary enlistment.*

1. What is your name? — 1. Surname PARK (BLOCK CAPITALS) Other names William Abernethy
2. Where were you born? — 2. In or near the town of Brisbane, In the State or country of Q'sland
3. Are you a natural born or a naturalised British Subject? If the latter, papers are to be produced — 3. Yes
4. What is your age and date of birth? — 4. Age 22 yrs, Date of Birth 23/8/20
5. What is your trade or occupation? — 5. Student
6. Are you married, single or widower? — 6. single
7. Give details of previous Military Service — 7. Q108364 Sgt, OTHER MILITARY SERVICE
8. If now serving, give particulars 30 Lisburn St, East Brisbane — 8. No. Rank Unit
9. Who is your actual next of kin? (Order of relationship:—wife, eldest son, eldest daughter, father, mother, eldest brother, eldest sister, eldest half-brother, eldest half-sister.) — 9. Name John Park, Address, Relationship Father
10. What is your permanent address? — 10.
11. What is your religious denomination? (Answer optional.) — 11. C of E
12. Have you ever been convicted by a civil court? — 12. No
13. Have you any of the following Educational Qualifications? If so, which? — 1. Certificate for Entry to Secondary School; 2. Intermediate; 3. Leaving; 4. Leaving Honours; 5. Technical; 6. University Degrees; 7. Other Diplomas

TERMINATION

APPOINTMENT

I, William Abernethy Park do solemnly declare that the above answers made by me to the above questions are true and that I am willing to serve in the Australian Military Forces within or beyond the limits of the Commonwealth.

Witnessed by J. Holkingworth S/Sgt. (Signature of Attesting or Witnessing Officer) Park (Signature)

* The person will be warned that should he give false answers to any of these questions he will be liable to heavy penalties under the Defence Act.

B MEDICAL EXAMINATION

I certify the above-named person to be fit for Class A1 ~~Temporarily unfit~~ Unfit (Signature)

C OATH OF ENLISTMENT †

I, William Abernethy Park swear that I will well and truly serve our Sovereign Lord, the King, in the Military Forces of the Commonwealth of Australia until the cessation of the present time of war and twelve months thereafter or until sooner lawfully discharged, dismissed or removed, and that I will resist His Majesty's enemies and cause His Majesty's peace to be kept and maintained, and that I will in all matters appertaining to my service faithfully discharge my duty according to law.

So help me God

Signature of Person Enlisted X Park

Subscribed at Brisbane in the State of Q'land this Fourth day of February 1943

Before me— Signature of Attesting Officer Capt

† Persons who object to take an oath may make an affirmation in accordance with the Third Schedule of the Defence Act. In such case the above form will be amended accordingly and initialled by the Attesting Officer.

D.3994/4.41.—C.4971 By Authority: H. E. Daw, Government Printer, Melbourne.

Figure 4 Bill Park's Attestation Form when he enlisted in the AIF. (National Archives)

Service and Casualty Form

The Service and Casualty Form details the movements, transfers, promotions, sicknesses, casualties etc during the soldier's service, from the time of his enlistment to discharge. Whilst it may seem that it is not particularly important for the entry of data onto the *WW2NR*, it is very good supportive evidence for both enlistment forms and the

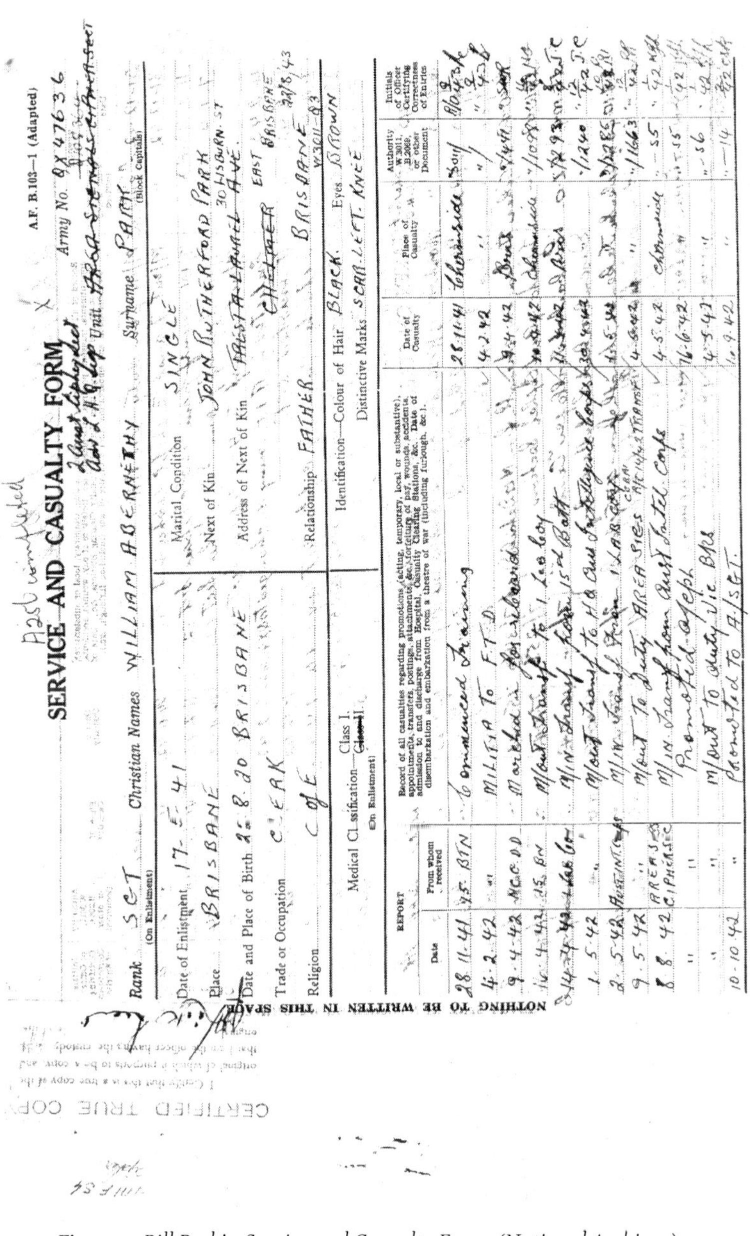
A.F. B.103—1 (Adapted)

SERVICE AND CASUALTY FORM

Army No. QX 47636

Rank SGT (On Enlistment) Christian Names WILLIAM ABERNETHY Surname PARK (Block Capitals)

Date of Enlistment 17-5-41

Place BRISBANE

Date and Place of Birth 25-8-20 BRISBANE

Trade or Occupation CLERK

Religion C of E

Medical Classification—Class I (On Enlistment)

Marital Condition SINGLE

Next of Kin JOHN RUTHERFORD PARK

Address of Next of Kin 30 LISBURN ST EAST BRISBANE

Relationship FATHER

Identification—Colour of Hair BLACK Eyes BROWN

Distinctive Marks SCAR LEFT KNEE

NOTHING TO BE WRITTEN IN THIS SPACE

Report Date	From whom received	Record of all casualties regarding promotions, appointments, transfers, postings, etc.	Date of Casualty	Place of Casualty
28.11.41	25 BTN	Commenced training	28.11.41	Chermside
4.2.42	"	MILITIA TO F.T.D.	4.2.42	"
9.4.42	HQ O.D.	Marched in for reboard	9.4.42	[illegible]
16.4.42	25 BN	M/out transf to 1 L.A.A. Coy	16.4.42	Chermside
14.4.42	1 LAA Coy	M/in transf from 15 Batt	[illegible]	[illegible]
1.5.42	"	M/out transf to HQ [illegible]	[illegible]	[illegible]
2.5.42	[illegible]	M/in transf from 1 LAA Coy	1.5.42	"
9.5.42		M/out to duty AREA SIGS	4.5.42	
8.8.42	AREA SIGS CIPHER SEC	M/in transf from [illegible] Corps	4.5.42	Chermside
"	"	Promoted A/Cpl	16.6.42	"
"	"	M/out to duty Vic BAR	4.5.42	"
10.10.42	"	Promoted to A/SGT	10.9.42	

CERTIFIED TRUE COPY

Figure 5 Bill Park's Service and Casualty Form. (National Archives)

discharge forms. It is possibly a source of information for the date and rank on discharge, but not for the unit on discharge.

Discharge papers

These papers started the rather complex procedure of discharging a soldier. It was another occasion when the army required soldiers to fill in forms with information they had already supplied during their service. It gives a snapshot view of the person and his or her service. A copy of Bill's 'Proceedings for Termination of an Officer's Appointment' is presented here. A similar form was used for other ranks. It is probably from this form that the information for 'posting at discharge' was obtained.

There are two items of particular interest. The first is 'Date commenced F.T.D'. The soldier wrote 28/11/41—the date army

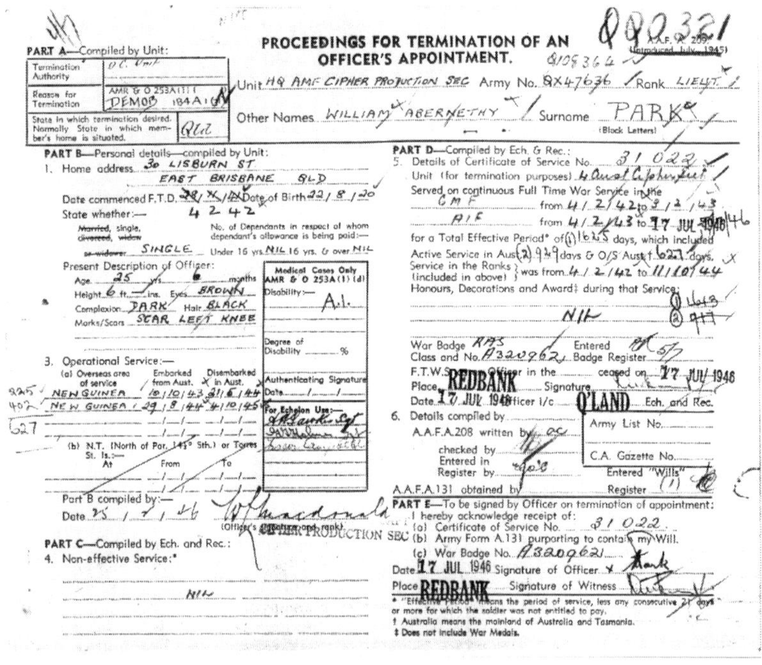

Q Q 2321

A.A.F. A. 209 (Introduced July, 1945)

PROCEEDINGS FOR TERMINATION OF AN OFFICER'S APPOINTMENT.

Q105364

PART A—Compiled by Unit:

Termination Authority	O.C. Unit
Reason for Termination	AMR & O 253A(1)(t) DEMOB 184A(1)(d)
State in which termination desired. Normally State in which member's home is situated.	Qld

Unit HQ AMF CIPHER PRODUCTION SEC Army No. QX47636 Rank LIEUT.

Other Names WILLIAM ABERNETHY Surname PARK (Block Letters)

PART B—Personal details—compiled by Unit:

1. Home address 30 LISBURN ST EAST BRISBANE QLD

Date commenced F.T.D. 28/XI/41 4 2 42 Date of Birth 22/8/20

State whether:— ~~Married~~, single, ~~divorced~~, ~~widow~~ ~~or widower~~ SINGLE

No. of Dependants in respect of whom dependant's allowance is being paid:— Under 16 yrs. NIL 16 yrs. & over NIL

Present Description of Officer:

Age 25 yrs. 6 months

Height 6 ft. — ins. Eyes BROWN

Complexion DARK Hair BLACK

Marks/Scars SCAR LEFT KNEE

Medical Cases Only AMR & O 253A(1)(d)

Disability:— A.1.

Degree of Disability ___ %

Authenticating Signature

Date / /

For Echelon Use:—

3. Operational Service:—

(a) Overseas area of service / Embarked from Aust. / Disembarked in Aust.

225 NEW GUINEA 10/10/43 21/6/44

402 NEW GUINEA 29/8/44 4/10/45

627

(b) N.T. (North of Par. 14½° Sth.) or Torres St. Is.:— At / From / To

Part B compiled by:—

Date 25/7/46 (Officer's signature and rank)

CIPHER PRODUCTION SEC

PART C—Compiled by Ech. and Rec.:

4. Non-effective Service:*

NIL

PART D—Compiled by Ech. & Rec.:

5. Details of Certificate of Service No. 31022

Unit (for termination purposes) 4 Aust Cipher Sect

Served on continuous Full Time War Service in the CMF from 4/2/42 to 3/2/43

AIF from 4/2/43 to 17 JUL 1946

for a Total Effective Period* of (1) 1625 days, which included Active Service in Aust† (2) 949 days & O/S Aust† 627 days.

Service in the Ranks (included in above) was from 4/2/42 to 11/10/44

Honours, Decorations and Award‡ during that Service: NIL

(1) 1643

(2) 977

War Badge Class and No. RAS A320962 Entered Badge Register

F.T.W.S. Officer in the ... ceased on 17 JUL 1946

Place REDBANK Signature

Date 17 JUL 1946 Officer i/c Q'LAND Ech. and Rec.

6. Details compiled by

A.A.F.A.208 written by OC

checked by

Entered in Register by

A.A.F.A.131 obtained by

Army List No.

C.A. Gazette No.

Entered "Wills" Register (1)

PART E—To be signed by Officer on termination of appointment:

I hereby acknowledge receipt of:

(a) Certificate of Service No. 31022

(b) Army Form A.131 purporting to contain my Will.

(c) War Badge No. A320621

Date 17 JUL 1946 Signature of Officer

Place REDBANK Signature of Witness

* "Effective Period" means the period of service, less any consecutive 21 days or more for which the soldier was not entitled to pay.

† Australia means the mainland of Australia and Tasmania.

‡ Does not include War Medals.

Figure 6 The Proceedings for Termination of an Officer's Appointment Form provides a snapshot view of Bill Park and his army service. (National Archives)

service started going into camp and when army pay started. Later (unbeknown to the soldier) someone altered the date to 4/2/42, which was the date he was 'converted' to full-time duty. The second item is the 'Total Effective Period' of 1625 days which was calculated from 4/2/42, of which 'active service' was 929 days in Australia and 627 days overseas (a total of 1556 days), sixty-nine days less than the Total Effective Period. So, that indicates that the soldier moved from inactive service to active service sixty-nine days from 4 February 1942, that is, on 14 April 1942. Why and how? Bill did not know that until recently. The answer is that Australia was declared by government proclamation to be an active service area from that latter date. So, service in (or with) an infantry battalion from November 1941 to early April, and part of the forces defending Brisbane from possible enemy attack was not considered active service. However, from 14 April 1942, service at Victoria Barracks, was active service.

No army service record?

Without the army service record, it would impossible to enter much of the information needed to complete the entry onto the *WW2NR*. As will be seen, there are other records that could have provided most of the information required. Either that was not realised at the time, or perhaps it was decided that looking for those other records would materially delay the introduction of the *WW2NR*.

Army records held by National Archives Office at Cannon Hill, Brisbane

The Brisbane office holds a number of army enlistment registers, cards and microfilm. There are two microfilms recording the names of all Queenslanders (male and female) who had enlisted in the army during World War 2. This record is in alphabetical order by name of serviceman/woman and shows name and army service number(s). It seems the microfilms were photographed from many thousands of index 'strips', which, apparently, are still held in the archives. The index strips themselves were presumably prepared from the enlistment registers. There are a number of large loose-leaf, handwritten master enlistment registers, a separate series for each series of army numbers, for example, AIF (QX), CMF or militia (Q), permanent army (QP) etc. The following notes refer to the CMF registers, but are generally applicable to the other registers.

The first Q enlistment register starts with the number Q1, ending up with a register with Q numbers above Q300000. However, that does not mean that more than 300 000 militia enlistments were recorded in Queensland in WW2. There were many cases where a Q number was not allocated, and is the main reason so many Q service numbers were not recorded on the *WW2NR*. The purpose of the enlistment register was to allocate a unique Q service number to each enlisted recruit and to ensure that there were no duplications. Against each number the name of the soldier was written, followed by the registered number of his pay book and sometimes, brief notes about the soldier. If the soldier later enlisted in the AIF, there was usually a reference to his QX number (which, of course, had been previously entered in the QX register). The enlistment registers did not usually attempt to follow the soldier's service after he enlisted, though, on occasions, there were some notations of interest. It seemed that many of the numbers below Q99000 were for voluntary enlistments in the militia when they got caught up in a new numbering system in 1940 and 1941. Perhaps a new method of recording pay on a centralised system may have had something to do with it too. It also seemed that many of the numbers above Q99000 were for new enlistments and call-ups for military training after 1940.

Pay records

In Queensland and, perhaps, elsewhere until after WW2, employees' wages had to be paid in cash each payday. Preparing for the payday was a major task for an employer: calculating each employee's pay, going to the bank to withdraw the total pay in the required mix of notes and coins, returning to the office to sort the money into pay packets and then handing the pay packet to the right employee. It was not unusual for the army in the prewar days to follow much the same procedure for its payments to the militia. Payments were made in cash to the militiamen on a drill night (thus encouraging attendance also) and the pay was signed for on a master pay sheet.

After the war started, there was a switch to a centralised accounting system and the issue of an individual paybook (something like a savings passbook); pay was credited to a soldier's paybook and any withdrawals were debited to it. This substantially reduced the problem of obtaining large amounts of cash from a bank each payday and distributing it among the troops. It virtually eliminated the payday parades—soldiers could make withdrawals from their paybooks at their units when they wanted some cash. The paybook became a soldier's most important possession; each one had an individual number and losing it was almost as bad a crime as losing a rifle. It also recorded other personal details and, in effect, became their universal passport as well. The paybook held by the soldier was regularly updated by the unit pay office; in addition, a ledger paycard for each soldier was kept at army finance or accounts headquarters and regularly updated from unit returns.

The new system for the militia was introduced in 1940. Existing militiamen were brought 'on line' and were given new army (Q) numbers in place of the peacetime numbers. As mentioned previously, a master enlistment register was kept at army headquarters in each military district (state or territory) in which was recorded the recruit's name, his new militia number and the number imprinted on the cover of his paybook. It was a massive undertaking, even though ledger (accounting) machines were used in the centralised accounting offices. It was completed in Queensland by May 1941.

Paycards held by the National Archives of Australia—Queensland (NAAQ)

NAAQ has a large collection of paycards for most of the army enlistments in Queensland for World War 2, filed in order of army

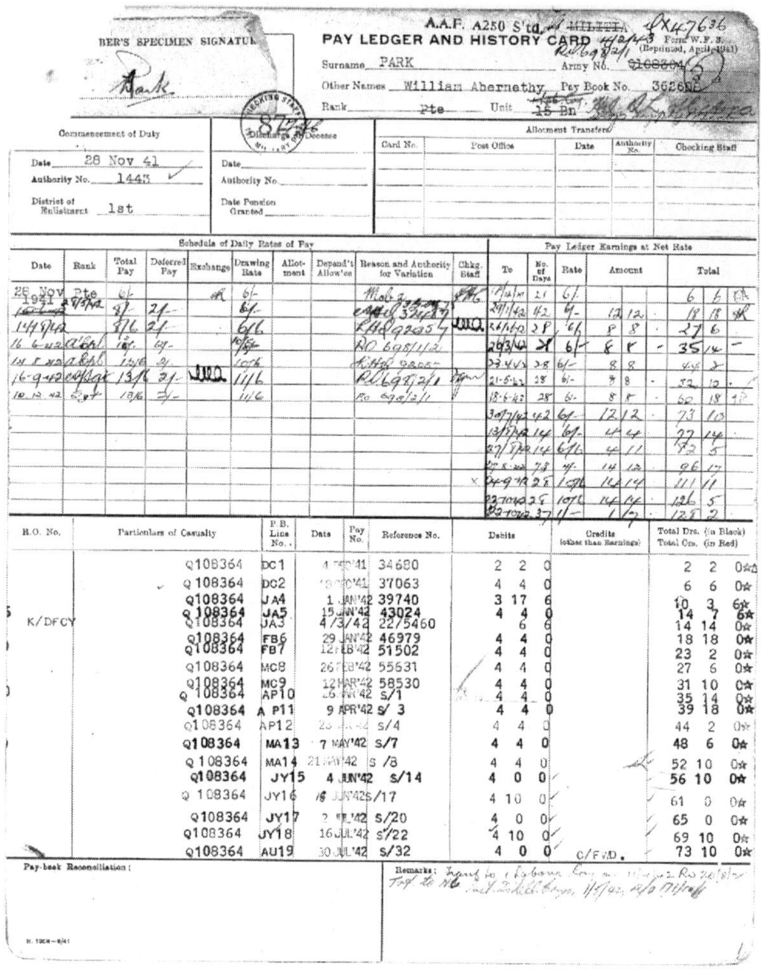

A.A.F. A250 S'td. QX47636

PAY LEDGER AND HISTORY CARD Form W.F. 3. (Reprinted, April 1941)

Surname PARK Army No. Q108364

Other Names William Abernethy Pay Book No. 36268

Rank Pte Unit 15 Bn

Commencement of Duty	Discharge or Decease
Date 28 Nov 41	Date
Authority No. 1443	Authority No.
District of Enlistment 1st	Date Pension Granted

Allotment Transfers

Card No.	Post Office	Date	Authority No.	Checking Staff

Schedule of Daily Rates of Pay

Date	Rank	Total Pay	Deferred Pay	Exchange	Drawing Rate	Allotment	Depend't's Allow'ce	Reason and Authority for Variation	Chkg. Staff
28 Nov 1941	Pte	6/-			6/-				

Pay Ledger Earnings at Net Rate

To	No. of Days	Rate	Amount	Total

R.O. No.	Particulars of Casualty	P.B. Line No.	Date	Pay No.	Reference No.	Debits	Credits (other than Earnings)	Total Drs. (in Black) Total Crs. (in Red)
	Q108364	DC1	4 DEC'41		34680	2 2 0		2 2 0
	Q108364	DC2	18 DEC'41		37063	4 4 0		6 6 0
	Q108364	JA4	1 JAN'42		39740	3 17 6		10 3 6
	Q108364	JA5	15 JAN'42		43024	4 4 0		14 7 6
K/DFCY	Q108364	JA3	4/3/42		2275460	6 6		14 14 0
	Q108364	FB6	29 JAN'42		46979	4 4 0		18 18 0
	Q108364	FB7	12 FEB'42		51502	4 4 0		23 2 0
	Q108364	MC8	26 FEB'42		55631	4 4 0		27 6 0
	Q108364	MC9	12 MAR'42		58530	4 4 0		31 10 0
	Q108364	AP10	26 MAR'42		S/1	4 4 0		35 14 0
	Q108364	AP11	9 APR'42		S/3	4 4 0		39 18 0
	Q108364	AP12	23 APR'42		S/4	4 4 0		44 2 0
	Q108364	MA13	7 MAY'42		S/7	4 4 0		48 6 0
	Q108364	MA14	21 MAY'42		S/8	4 4 0		52 10 0
	Q108364	JY15	4 JUN'42		S/14	4 0 0		56 10 0
	Q108364	JY16	18 JUN'42		S/17	4 10 0		61 0 0
	Q108364	JY17	2 JUL'42		S/20	4 0 0		65 0 0
	Q108364	JY18	16 JUL'42		S/22	4 10 0		69 10 0
	Q108364	AU19	30 JUL'42		S/32	4 0 0	C/FWD.	73 10 0

Pay-book Reconciliation:

Remarks:

Figure 7 *Bill Park's first paycard (National Archives)*

service number. So, first it was necessary to find out the soldier's service number and, if he had more than one, under which number the paycards might be filed. Usually, it is under the number of the last enlistment. A copy of Bill Park's first paycard as Q108364 appears here. It was not filed under that number, but under QX47636 which was his later service number.

In addition to containing pay details, the paycard also had a variety of additional notes recorded on it. It was usually headed up with the full name of the soldier, his army number, the first unit to which he had been allocated and, most important of all, the date from which he had been paid—in other words, the actual date he had been taken on strength (gone into camp).

At first glance, it seemed that a lot of cards were not held, but it soon became apparent that if the soldier had transferred to the AIF, or had re-enlisted, then the card had been assigned to his new number. Fortunately, if it was to a QX number, then it was almost certain that the paycard would be under that number. But, it grew even more complicated. If the soldier had first enlisted in the AIF, been discharged and then later enlisted in the militia, he would be given a Q number and the pay records might be filed under that number, or they might be found under the two separate numbers. Some pay records could not be found under either number. They, possibly, were in respect of soldiers who moved to the postwar army, in which case they were given yet another number (or numbers) under which the records were filed. It was sometimes very difficult to follow the trail. Some paycards could not be found at all.

Summary

The complete contextual service records of many of the soldiers not recorded on the *WW2NR* were apparently destroyed years ago, long before the *WW2NR* was even thought about. Consequently, there are no remnant records to show what enlistment forms they signed. Hence, it cannot be proved that they signed up for army service and, if so, when and whether for the duration of the war, full-time duty or what. Crucially, the sources of testimony—the soldiers themselves—are disappearing too.

Someone, somewhere, some time ago made the decision that if a man had been in the army, but had not signed the 'acceptable' enlistment form, then his name would not be entered on the *WW2NR*. The fact that other records (e.g. paycards and enlistment registers) show army service seems to have been ignored. Who made those decisions and why are they not explained in the explanatory memorandum about the *WW2NR*?

Conclusions

The *WW2NR* is not a reliable source of information about the service of many Australian soldiers of that era, and this lack of a reliable archive hinders many in the community—especially journalists compiling anniversary supplements—from obtaining accurate information about past warriors. The evident lack of accurate information about our past warriors challenges the official position that the *WW2NR* is a virtual war memorial, and also challenges the government's statements that former soldiers are adequately memorialised.

We have noted that the work done by the contractor (based on the methodology published on the *WW2NR* website) appears to have been insufficient, but we also note that what was done was not wrong—it just did not go far enough. The commissioning body should have asked for a two-step tender process: the first being to transfer historical data from paper records to computer, 'warts and all'. This was done. But once the data was online, it needed to be carefully audited by people who could supply the context and the testimony which our research suggests was integral to arriving at a completely error free archive. This requires different people with different skills, and in the case of the *WW2NR*, they would have to be drawn from a rapidly decreasing segment of the population: the Diggers themselves. However, with computerisation and distributed networks such as the Internet, the work can be done anywhere in the country or the world. All it needs is the will and resources to do it.

The real problem with the *WW2NR* lies not so much with the original contractors but with those who have followed, in not continuing with proper verification of the computer data on a systematic basis.

Authors' note

The identity of 'Source X', a government source of information, has been deleted from this book as the individual spoke on condition of anonymity.

Notes

1. The literature on this is abundant but we found a quick and useful summary on this accountancy website, < http://www.canhamrogers.com/HDEB.htm>.
2. A confidential source
3. < www.WW2roll.gov.au>
4. < www.naa.gov.au>

References

Commonwealth of Australia 2002, *World War 2 Nominal Roll*, viewed 25 March 09, <http://www.ww2roll.gov.au/doc/about.asp#dataprocess>.

Edy, J 1999, 'Journalistic Uses of Collective Memory', *Journal of Communication*, Spring 1999, pp. 71–85.

Gibson, J & Dell, A 1989, *Tudor and Stuart Muster Rolls*, Federation of Family History Societies, viewed February 2009, <http://www.ffhs.org.uk/>.

Heraldry and Genealogy Society of Canberra Inc 2009, *Graves and Memorials of Australians in the Boer War 1899–1902*, viewed March 2009, <www.hagsoc.org.au/sagraves/>.

Hope, V 2003, 'Trophies and tombstones; commemorating the Roman soldier', *World Archaeology*, vol. 35, no. 1, pp. 79–97.

Inglis, KS 2005, *Sacred Places – War Memorials in the Australian Landscape* Melbourne University Press, Melbourne.

Mackay, H 2008, *Advance Australia Where?*, Hachette, Sydney.

Meyer, P 2004, *The Vanishing Newspaper, Saving Journalism in the Information Age*, University of Missouri Press, Missouri, pp. 83–108.

Olick J & Robbins, J 1998, *Annual Review of Sociology*, vol. 24, pp. 105–115.

Park, W 2009, *Australia's World War 2 Nominal Roll: accurate record or true record?*, VDM Verlag Dr. Müller Aktiengesellschaft & Co. KG, Saarbrücken, Germany.

Thelen, D 1989, 'Memory and American History', Journal of American History, vol. 75, no. 4, pp. 1117–1129.

Whitmarsh, A 2001, '"We Will Remember Them" Memory and Commemoration in War Museums"', *Journal of Conservation and Museum Studies*, no. 7, pp. 1–15.

Chapter 8

Viridian: Mostar 2004

Richard Chew
University of South Australia

Life was created along the Neretva River. Were it not for the Neretva, there would be no Mostar. The River is the giver of life. In order to cross over it, a bridge was born.

Esina Babović, citizen of Mostar, in Blakstad 2000

October 2004

We arrive in Mostar at around 2pm, after a hair-raising trip in a borrowed Mercedes through the mountainous valley of the Neretva River. It is a clear autumn day, and there is a bite in the air. I pity the divers who will jump from the Old Bridge this afternoon. The Neretva is icy-cold, even at the height of summer, when the annual diving contest is held in July, as it has been for hundreds of years.

Figure 1 *Stari Most, the Old Bridge, Mostar, Bosnia-Herzegovina. (author's photo)*

Local alpha males swan dive from Stari Most, the spectacular Ottoman bridge which spans the narrow gorge at the heart of the city and for a night, the winner becomes the 'boss' of Mostar, and a real hit with the ladies. When they are not competing, the divers hang out in their clubhouse, or dive for tourists for as much as fifty Euros a time. Expensive? Perhaps; but this is a risky business. The bridge rises to twenty-four metres at its apex. It is a leap of faith and requires supreme courage and perfect technique.

I am here to research and collect material for an oratorio, a musical biography of the bridge and its significance as a symbol for the local community. I'm travelling with my collaborators on this project; theatre-maker Graeme Rose, writer Peter Cann and Bosnian actor Mirsad Solaković, who has agreed to accompany us as translator.

We hastily deposit our gear at our lodgings and head straight for the old town, making our way through the shell-scarred buildings to the banks of the Neretva and our first glimpse of the bridge.

As we reach the natural amphitheatre beneath the arch, I am immediately struck by the colour of the river and the speed of the current. The water is a deep green, a true viridian, quite unlike anything I've seen before. The river swirls and eddies, forming tiny whirlpools which twist and disperse at an alarming rate. Suddenly, I have even more respect for the young men who hurl themselves from the parapet of the bridge for a fistful of Euros.

And there it is. Stari Most, a jewel of Ottoman architecture, celebrated in the poems of the Sufis and in the beautiful local songs of the region, the Sevda Linka, which animate the heart of every Mostarian. Except all this is an illusion. The bridge is a copy, a perfect replica of its predecessor, a phoenix arisen from the flames of war. It is beautiful, of course, but it is too new, too clean.

At 10.15am on 9 November 1993[1], Stari Most was obliterated by Croatian artillery at the height of the Bosnian War. It was a deliberate act of urbicide[2], the pre-meditated destruction of significant religious and cultural artefacts, aligned to an ultra-nationalist policy of ethnic cleansing. For more than four hundred years, Stari Most had stood as a symbol of peaceful co-existence between the various ethnic and religious communities within the region. For nationalists, however, the bridge represented Islamic fundamentalism. The architect of its destruction was Major-General Slobodan Praljak, commander of the Croatian Defence Council (HVO), who, in peacetime had worked in television and theatre as a director, as well as lecturing in philosophy and psychology at the University of Zagreb. His opus magnum, if one could call it such, was certainly theatrical, a spectacle which was captured live on camera and evoked universal condemnation from the international community.

That a high-profile intellectual, an artist and philosopher, could be capable of such an act is shocking. Unfortunately, the ability to appreciate art does not predispose the capacity for empathy. Consider Reinhard Heydrich, one of the principal architects of Hitler's Final Solution, who emerged from a cultured, musical family and was himself an exceptional violinist. As George Steiner warned: 'We know that a man can read Goethe and Rilke in the evening, can play Bach and Schubert and go to his day's work at Auschwitz in the morning' (1963, p. ix).

With *Stari Most*, I had come to a point in my own creative work where I was beginning to ask some challenging questions about the role of music as a catalyst for social change. I wanted to explore the possibility of a secular oratorio, which, in its subject matter, dealt unequivocally with a specific conflict.

On 23 July 2004, the day on which the new Stari Most was officially opened, I was performing a large-scale community music-theatre work called *Unearth; Stories of a War* at the Midland Arts Centre (MAC) in Birmingham, UK. The piece was commissioned by MAC and created as a collaboration between theatre maker Graeme Rose, director Steve Johnstone and writer Peter Cann. I was both composer and musical director. *Unearth* was concerned with the exhumation of mass graves in Bosnia in the aftermath of the war (1991–93) and the efforts of forensic pathologists at the mortuary in Tuzla to establish the identity of the victims.

The text was an amalgam of original material by Cann and extracts from a series of interviews with members of the Bosnian diaspora living in Birmingham. I remember feeling a profound sense of unease before accepting the commission. At the time, I had little knowledge of the complex political situation that had ignited the conflict in the former Yugoslavia and felt that we were in danger of appropriating the suffering of others in the name of art. However, once the process of devising the work began, my initial reticence began to dissipate. The Bosnian people we spoke to and worked with on this project were, without exception, eager to participate and felt compelled to tell their stories. It represented an opportunity for their pain and suffering to be acknowledged and shared by their adopted community. This is a common response among survivors of conflict. The American psychologist Robert J Lifton describes it in the following way:

> In this effort to give form to their feelings, they show the survivor's need to achieve a new sense of self and world. They take on the survivor mission of telling their tale, and they tell it with rare intensity and moral force. Their truth must be shared; others must be enabled to participate in their survivor experience and, above all, to share the guilt and responsibility. Telling the tale is a political act. (in Langer 1978, p. 24)

Several things happened during the planning and performance of *Unearth* which I believe to be significant in the context of this chapter:

- The community, as it became known. This consisted of professional actors, singers and musicians, a primary school choir and community performers. For the duration of their involvement in the project, they became the custodians and curators of a repository of knowledge and testimony, a situation that was, for many, a new and challenging experience.

- One of the professional performers, a young Bosnian actor called Mirsad Solaković, became a touchstone for the rest of the cast. As a child, he had lived through some of the worst moments of the war, including the ethnic cleansing of his own village and the brutal violence of Serb militiamen. Mirsad's own story was told in the piece, and, in a way, this alone was a sufficient justification for its existence.
- The bringing of these testimonies, these stories, into the light in the form of performance, allowed the *Unearth* community to participate in the 'survivor experience' and share the burden of responsibility. For many people, this was a profoundly moving experience and a rare privilege, a chance to act rather than simply observe the war from a distance.
- The production initiated events which none of us who created the piece could have imagined. For example, as a result of the interviews conducted in Tuzla during the development of the project, the research lab became aware of the small but significant community of Bosnian Muslims living in the West Midlands, and pledged to send a representative to collect DNA for identity matching back in Bosnia. The idea that a piece of music-theatre could possibly become a catalyst for even one of these people locating a lost member of their family was both humbling and inspiring.

Unearth created the ideological and conceptual framework for *Stari Most*. Peter Cann and I decided to collaborate again and we made an initial research trip to Mostar in the autumn of 2004. It became clear in our conversations with the citizens of Mostar that the re-construction of Stari Most, whilst it had been an important symbolic gesture on the part of the international community, had done little to alleviate the deep divisions which now defined the infrastructure of the city. Peter described the situation in the following way in his libretto:

For there are two towns where once was one.
Separate hospitals and separate schools.
The bridge is lovely, but not the same,
A stitch in an unhealed wound ...

Stari Most has been celebrated as a cultural icon for over 400 years. In many ways, the oratorio represents continuation of this tradition; it is, quite literally, a love song to the old bridge.

October 2004
We stand beneath the bridge at dusk and marvel, as so many have done that such a thing as this is possible. Already, in the recesses of my mind, I can hear a distant music: two voices, a counterpoint between the river, the life-giver and the bridge, the lover. Diving from this bridge is a ritual, a rite of passage for the young men of Mostar, which confirms this umbilical connection. I need to capture the essence of this act of becoming in music.

Stari Most is essentially a love story, told through a sequence of letters between the two protagonists, Alma and Dino. He is Croatian Catholic; she is a Bosniak, a Bosnian Muslim. Together they represent the two faiths and cultures that were driven into such bitter enmity during the brutal disintegration of former Yugoslavia, and, on a more elemental level, they are a metaphor for the bridge and the river, man and woman. Their relationship is never consummated. They remain separate, 'never lovers, ever friends', despite the 'vile convulsion' of a war which threatens to destroy them both.

In his libretto, Peter Cann manages to juxtapose the story of Alma and Dino's relationship, (conveyed through their correspondence) against the narrative backdrop of the building of Stari Most, its destruction and reconstruction after the war. The opening of the work is particularly striking, in its evocation of the way in which bridges came into the world and how the first bridge was built:

God made the round world smooth
With no flaw to mar its beauty
But Satan in the night
Scratched upon it in his malice

He rent the ragged gorge
And his nails scraped out the valleys
So when the angels woke
All their weeping filled the rivers

And so, from bank to bank
They formed great arches with their pinions
That from that time
Mankind would know that they must build bridges

As wings of angels
As wings of angels

This is a poetic version of a story told by Alihodja, an elderly Muslim, in Ivo Andric's novel *The Bridge on the Drina* (1977, pp. 208–209). It sets the broader, mythic landscape of the bridge as a metaphor for spiritual communication, the meta-narrative which underpins the human connection between Alma and Dino.

Of the challenges that faced us during the writing of *Stari Most*, the most critical was the question of what form the voice of the old bridge should take. Lucy Blakstad quotes Esina, a resident of Mostar as saying: 'The old bridge was something special, like a person with an exceptional soul, with all the nice qualities a man should have' (Blakstad 2002, p. 158). This personification of the bridge is something that comes up time and time again in the eye-witness accounts of the final moments of its destruction.

When Peter Cann and I visited Mostar, we were introduced to Mirsad Pasić (Deda), one of the great Mostar bridge divers. We sat with him

Figure 2 *Mirsad Pasić (Deda), one of the most famous Mostar bridge divers. (author's photo)*

in the bright sunshine at a café on the west side of the bridge near the divers club. Deda was a man with a large presence in the community. A steady stream of Mostar residents made their way across the bridge, greeting him in deference as they passed. His voice was like gravel, a deep growl formed through many years of chain-smoking. During our conversation, a group of schoolchildren, including Deda's eight-year-old granddaughter, came singing across the bridge. I captured the moment on my mini-disc. Instantly, it became clear to us that the voice of Stari Most in our piece should be assigned to a children's choir. I was reminded of a poem about the desire for peace in Northern Ireland, written by a twelve-year-old boy, Sean McLaughlin, shortly before his death in the 1998 Omagh Bombing:

Orange and Green, it doesn't matter
United now, don't shatter our dream

Scatter the seeds of peace over our land
So we can travel hand in hand
Across a bridge of hope.[3]

The bridge choir in Stari Most is both a character, with a defined voice of its own and a narrator. A mixture of girls and boys voices creates a quality of 'otherness' which is matched in the text and music. This is not one voice, but many; it is not specified in terms of gender; it has a particular timbre quite unlike that of the two adult soloists. There is something primal about children's voices. Between the ages of roughly eight and twelve, children of both sexes produce a clear, ringing sound with no vibrato. I wanted to capture this almost pre-conscious sonority in the music of the bridge choir from the outset, and so I gave them a nonverbal vocalisation at the beginning of the work; Ee oo ee oo, Ha! Ee oo ee oo, Hoo! :

The melody is primitive and modal, an oscillation between C#, G and the key-note E. Here, we have a symbol which has resonated through the history of western music, the dissonant interval of the tritone, the *diabolus in musica* or devil's interval. The bridge choir then intones the story of the origin of bridges, accompanied by a drone in the lower strings and heavy, ritualistic percussion.

Whilst the bridge choir narrates the story of Stari Most, from its inception in 1566 to its demise in 1993, their function within the piece is to embody a vision of hope; they are the spirit of the bridge, an expression of its essence. Ultimately, the rebuilding of Mostar can only truly begin in the hearts and minds of its children. Again, Peter Cann distils this idea beautifully in the libretto. The bridge choir sings:

I am more than stone
I am every hand that touched me
I am every foot
That pressed upon my spine
Every soul, every sole
I can be dreamed again

The voice of the bridge is an archetype, a character that narrates its own life story in the first person, but also acts as a carrier frequency for the dreams and aspirations of the community that created it. It absorbs their fictions, which become embedded in the fabric of a collective memory. Ivo Andric describes this process in the following way in *The Bridge on the Drina*:

> men began to remember details and to embroider the creation of a real, skilfully built and lasting bridge with fabulous tales which they well knew how to weave and remember. (1977, p. 27)

At the beginning of *Stari Most*, Peter Cann establishes the concept of the bridge as a sentient being, which reflects upon the miracle of its own conception:

I was a triumph of hand and stone
An arch of implausible grace
From side to side
From East to West

From West to East
From day to day
A thousand souls
Stepped upon my slender spine

And subsequently contemplates the nature of its creator:

Who dreamed
Who dreamed these bold trajectories?
Two flung arcs each that hold the other
Through an urge to fall
Who dreamed this fragile equilibrium?

We are left in no doubt that the bridge is conscious of its own importance as a cultural icon, but Cann skilfully connects this idea of a broader, metaphysical significance with a description of the bridge's everyday function as a thoroughfare between east and west Mostar. When the text is repeated, a little later, Peter changes the final couplet to: *Mohammed and the Christ leaned upon my rail.* This shift of the linguistic lens from the everyday to the epic is one of the qualities that make this libretto so strong. With a remarkable economy of language, Peter conveys an image of the bridge as a spiritual node, the intersection for a discourse between Islam and Christianity, but undercuts this with the word 'leaned', giving us a picture of two local residents engaged in casual conversation.

Having established the mythic, symbolic and religious dimensions of the bridge itself, Cann focuses his attention on the domestic, interior world of Dino and Alma. He is living in exile, having deserted the army after the destruction of the bridge. Her tone in this first letter is assertive and confrontational; this is no shy and submissive Muslim woman. However, as the letter progresses, we sense her emotional warmth towards him, through the memory of their first kiss beneath the bridge:

You're not the first I kissed beneath the arch
And nor, my distant friend, were you the last
You're not the diver tattooed on my back
And yet that night is etched behind my eyes
The bridge above us pale against the dark
The stonework cold and rough against my back

The tree that grew out of the ancient wall
The spider's web that caught the moon
The glitter of the cross you wore
You always wore, though seldom went to mass

Dino, on the other hand, is still in denial about his role in the ethnic cleansing of Mostar. Whilst we are never made aware of what he did, it is clear that, for him, the memories are still too raw for him to contemplate returning to Bosnia. Only much later in the piece is he able to begin facing the demons of his past, when Alma informs him that she is learning to dive and will jump from the newly rebuilt bridge for him. Her challenge to his manhood is enough to wake him to his senses and return to Mostar to dive with her.

Dino's memory of his own rite of passage, his prize-winning dive from Stari Most required a musical response which illustrated the carnival-like atmosphere of the event and the preening machismo of the divers themselves. I found a perfect model for this in the testosterone-driven rhythms of Balkan brass band music, particularly as represented by Goran Bregovic's *Weddings and Funerals Band* and the Macedonian Kočani Orkestar.

The divers command a mythic status in Mostar. They are known as the *Ikari*, the Icaruses, a title which is reflected in the name of their exclusive club, the *Mostarski Ikari*, situated within the western tower of the bridge.

Figure 3 *A Mostar bridge diver prepares (author's photo)*

In the introduction to Dino's dive, the bridge choir establishes the atmosphere with an evocative song about the desire to fly:

Birdmen, birdmen
Perching on the ledge
Proud as Icarus
Poised upon the edge

The libretto is written with an innate sense of musical cadence. The meter of the text guided me, as composer, in a certain direction, where I was able to enhance the implied crescendo of the last seven lines in music. I also wanted to create a sense of location from a geographical point of view in the sound world, and I found a Macedonian folksong called *Stamena* which had a similar metric flow to the text. I did not use the melody itself, which is almost chanted on a monotone, but the instrumental introduction, which is played in a Turkish, highly ornamented style on clarinet and flute. My aim was not pastiche but an organic response to the words, which required assimilation of an unfamiliar musical style, spoken in my own compositional dialect.

Dino's dive is one of the focal points of *Stari Most*, a moment in which 'the world comes to a point'. His description of the seconds preceding the jump are pure theatre:

The stone was hot beneath my toes
The crowd was sitting at my feet
The breeze was licking at my skin
The sun is waiting at my back

And I was mighty

I stretch my arms from bank to bank
One scoop could gather this small crowd
And crush them all against my chest
I breathe them down into my lungs

And I was mighty

He is a colossus, as well as a desirable catch for the waiting crowd of girls below. The dive is a mating display, a demonstration of sexual fitness which is intended for Alma's eyes only. I timed the music of Dino's dive to match the dive that I had witnessed in Mostar. Dino shouts his physical preparation in counterpoint with a rising four-note theme from the bridge choir.

The orchestra then introduces a new melody, which begins in the violas and is subsequently taken up by the woodwinds. This is the theme associated with the Neretva, which I heard in my head while standing on the bridge, entranced by the rapid flow of the current and the extraordinary colour of the water below:

In a choral work of this scale, the orchestra has a special role to play, both as an accompaniment to the sung drama and as a character in its own right, commenting on and amplifying the narrative drive of the text. There are a number of short instrumental interludes in *Stari Most* which are there to provide a natural break in the flow of storytelling, allowing the audience to absorb and ingest the textual information whilst retaining the musical continuum. One of the most important moments in the piece in terms of orchestral music was the destruction of the bridge. I watched the video footage of the collapse of Stari Most again and again, wondering how it would be possible to represent this defining moment in music. I felt that the music should almost scream. All of the senseless, reckless violence of this conflict needed to be encoded in the sounds I chose. As Susan Sontag puts it:

> War tears, rends. War rips open, eviscerates. War scorches. War dismembers. War ruins. (2003, p. 7)

For the destruction of the bridge to work successfully, the musical material associated with the bridge needed to be harnessed in some sort of collision. Textually, also, the three voices of Alma, Dino and the Bridge choir are drawn together at this point and are eventually drowned out by the full orchestra.

Four musical themes meet each other head-on: a five-note chromatic melody which is heard in the woodwinds when Dino is about to perform his dive at the competition is juxtaposed with a theme in the brass, associated with the building of Stari Most at the beginning of the piece. It sounds like the ringing of bells or a medieval organum, and, at this point, it appears in an augmented form, slowed down as if in slow motion.

Against this, the piano plays a repeated group of six bravura chords, a grotesque parody of the opening of Tchaikovsky's First Piano Concerto. The chords are marked fortissimo in the score, and, as the full orchestral texture begins to subside, they continue, like large chunks of falling masonry.[4]

The final layer in this orchestral fabric is the fragile voice of the oboe, which is buried deep in the prevailing cacophony and is only heard briefly as the dust settles. This is a musical cryptogram, based on a chromatic alphabet. The nine-note melody spells out the name of Stari Most in music, thus:

This musical signature is inaudible, rather like the unseen carvings and sculptures in the recesses of cathedrals. It is an invisible detail, yet there is something about the visual contour of the melody which seems to represent the bridge, almost like a Kanji.

When I was writing the music for *Unearth*, I received a recording of a selection of Bosnian lullabies, sung *a cappella* by various unknown singers. One in particular caught my attention. It is called *Spavej Sine*

(Sleep, my Son) and is well known in the region.[5] I incorporated the song into the score of the third part of *Unearth*, which is modelled loosely on JS Bach's *St Matthew Passion*. The voice of this unknown woman seemed somehow lost in time. It was a fairly old field recording and there was no way of tracing her. The sound of her singing was at once very specific, rooted in her language and her culture and at the same time untrammelled, limitless. It seems to convey a universal sense of loss.

I was reminded of something Edward Said talks about in his Reith Lectures of 1993 (the year in which Stari Most was destroyed). He argues that the intellectual's responsibility is to 'represent collective suffering and testify to its travails'. He continues by saying that one must attempt to 'universalize the crisis, to give greater human scope to what a particular race or nation has suffered', and 'to associate that experience with the suffering of others' (Said 1994, pp. 43–44).

Stari Most is not a 'verbatim' art work, (as *Unearth* is, at least in part). It does not contain any primary data source material from interviews or recorded testimony. It is a fictional, poetic account of a specific trauma, an acknowledgement of the pain and suffering borne by a particular community, set within the wider frame of human experience in situations of conflict.

Being in Mostar was an intense experience which taught me about the emotional and spiritual significance of architecture. As Peter Bishop rightly says; 'the Mostar Bridge was experienced as something sacred to many. Here was a trace of ancient associations—the bridge as spiritual technology, as sacred architecture' (Bishop 2008, p. 161).

During my last trip to the UK in 2008, I revisited Coventry Cathedral, which, like the site in Mostar has become a symbol of rebirth and transformation in the aftermath of conflict. Unlike Stari Most, which was painstakingly reconstructed using original plans and Ottoman building techniques, the new cathedral at Coventry stands cheek-by-jowl with its burnt-out predecessor and is a paean to post-modernism. There are, however, a number of resonances which connect the two sites.

The first relates to the use of remnants or wreckage as a physical marker of past trauma. In the old cathedral at Coventry, one finds the Charred Cross. Shortly after the destruction, the cathedral stonemason, Jock Forbes, noticed that two of the burnt medieval roof timbers had fallen in the shape of a cross. He set them up in the ruins where they were later placed on an altar of rubble with the words 'Father Forgive' inscribed on the sanctuary wall. In Mostar, the remains of the original bridge were salvaged by divers from the river bed, but were too damaged to be used in the fabric of the reconstruction, so they have been placed as a permanent reminder of the tragedy in the natural amphitheatre beneath the new bridge.

Figure 4 Sections of the original Stari Most, salvaged from the river, laid to rest in the natural amphitheatre beneath the new bridge. (author's photo)

Figure 5 Reconciliation sculpture at Coventry Cathedral, by Josefina de Vasconcellos. (author's photo)

Within the shell of the old Coventry Cathedral, there stands a sculpture called *Reconciliation*, by Josefina de Vasconcellos.[6] It is an image of a man and a woman in an embrace and it forms a slender arch like the Stari Most. This symbol of human connection, an embrace which spans the divisions between race, religion, political ideology and culture is universal and immensely powerful. For me, it represents Alma and Dino.

When the new cathedral was consecrated in 1962, a specially commissioned choral work was performed to mark the event. This was Benjamin Britten's *War Requiem*, a universally acknowledged masterpiece in the oratorio repertory. In writing *Stari Most*, I have derived inspiration from Britten's exemplary word setting and innate sense of dramatic pace. *Stari Most* is not a religious piece, but it offers a message of consolation through the acknowledgement of suffering, and a belief in the possibility of hope in the face of overwhelming odds. As the poet Seamus Heaney reminds us:

> History says, 'Don't hope on this side of the grave'. But then, once in a lifetime the longed-for tidal wave of justice can rise up, and hope and history rhyme. So hope for a great sea-change on the far side of revenge. Believe that a further shore is reachable from here. Believe in miracles and cures and healing wells. (Heaney 1991, p. 78)

Notes

1. The date is significant, in that it was the 55th anniversary of *Kristallnacht.*
2. The term urbicide was first used by Marshall Berman in 1987, and has since been taken up by several writers in reference to violence perpetrated against the city. Peter Bishop refers to the destruction of Stari Most as 'ponticide', literally the murder of a bridge, a description which is supported in interviews with Mostar residents, who viewed the old bridge as a person who connected their city (Bishop 2008, pp. 157–161).
3. For more information about Sean McLaughlin's poem, see article at BBC Online, http://news.bbc.co.uk/1/hi/entertainment/206240.stm.
4. The virtuosity of this section also reflects ironically on the 'performance' of destruction.
5. The song appears in the opening titles of Daris Tanovic's film *No Man's Land* (2001).
6. An identical sculpture has been placed on behalf of the citizens of Coventry in the Peace Garden in Hiroshima, Japan. The inscription reads: 'Both sculptures remind us that, in the face of destructive forces, human dignity and love will triumph over disaster and bring nations together in respect and peace.'

References

Chew, R & Cann, P 2009, *Stari Most*, Choralworks Inc, Adelaide.

Andrić, I 1977, *The Bridge on the Drina*, University of Chicago Press, Chicago.

Barenboim, D & Said E 2004, *Parallels and Paradoxes: Explorations in Music and Society*, Vintage, New York.

Bishop, P 2008, *Bridge*, Reaktion Books Ltd, London.

Blakstad, L 2002, *Bridge: The Architecture of Connection*, August/Birkhäuser, London/Switzerland.

Heaney, S 1991, *The Cure at Troy: A version of Sophocles' Philoctetes*, Farrar, Strauss and Giraux, New York.

Langer, LL 1978, *The Age of Atrocity: Death in Modern Literature*, Beacon Press, Boston.

Said, E 1994, *Representation of the Intellectual: The 1993 Reith Lectures*, Vintage, London.

Sells, M A 1998, *The Bridge Betrayed: Religion and the Genocide in Bosnia*, University of California Press, Berkley.

Sontag, S 2003, *Regarding the Pain of Others*, Picador, New York.

Steiner, G 1967, *Language and Silence: Essays 1958-1962*, preface, Faber & Faber, New York.

Waterman, R 2008, *When Swan Lake comes to Sarajevo: A musician journeys into the aftermath of war*, Canterbury Press.

Contributors

Peter Bishop is Associate Professor in the School of Communication, International Studies and Languages at the University of South Australia. He has published widely on the areas of reconciliation, hope, memory, imagination, place and travel. Recent publications include: 'Reconciliation Travel & Writings of War', in *Writings of War*, eds. C Woods & J Timoney, Lythrum Press; 'The Shadow of Hope: Reconciliation & Imaginal Pedagogies', in *Pedagogies of the Imagination: Mythopoetic Curriculum in Educational Practice*, eds. T Leonard & P Willis, Springer; 'To Witness and Remember: Mapping Reconciliation Travel', in *Travel Writing, Form and Empire*, eds. J Kuehn and P Smethurst, Routledge.

Richard Chew is an internationally recognised composer, choral conductor, singer and pianist. His works include four operas, several large-scale compositions for chorus and orchestra and music for theatre and film. Richard's works have been premiered in the Vienna Festival, International Festival of Arts and Ideas, Connecticut, USA, Chor Biennale, Amsterdam, Bath International Music Festival, Three Choirs Festival, and at the New Victory Theatre on Broadway. He has worked with many of the foremost opera, theatre companies and classical ensembles in the UK, including the Royal Shakespeare Company, ROH Covent Garden, English National Opera, Welsh National Opera, The London Symphony Orchestra, London Sinfonietta and Lindsay Quartet. Richard is currently lecturer in Music and Drama at the University of South Australia, Musical Director of the Adelaide Harmony Choir, visiting lecturer in choral music at the Elder Conservatorium and a regular pre-concert speaker for the Adelaide Symphony Orchestra.

John Cokley PhD, Bachelor of Business, Grad Cert Education, worked as a reporter and feature writer, subeditor, trainer and website developer at News Corporation in Brisbane, Australia, between 1985 and 2002, after working for the *Daily Sun* newspaper and the Australian Associated Press wire service (1984–1985). He continues to maintain a level of professional practice in the private sector and is a member of the Society of Editors (Queensland), the Australasian Research Management Society and the Journalism Education Association (Australia). He began teaching journalism at universities after graduating with a bachelor's degree in business (communication) from the Queensland University of Technology (QUT) in 1990 as well as continuing to write for engineering, retail and indigenous magazines, books and newspapers. He was the first Journalist-in-Residence at Griffith University (2002), lectured in journalism at James Cook University, Townsville (2003–2004) and started lecturing and researching full-time at the University of Queensland in 2005.

Professor Kerry Philip Green is Head of the School of Communication, International Studies and Languages at the University of South Australia. He specialises in newspaper audience research, computer-assisted journalism, trauma and journalism, and news media organisation and management. Professor Green is project leader of a federal government-funded project investigating journalists' engagement with 'vulnerable' sources, which researches psychological trauma that difficult reporting assignments may cause to both journalists and their audience members. He also is part of a national research project, funded by the Department of Immigration and Citizenship, investigating the representation of ethnic diversity in Australia's news media. He is an executive member of Dart Australasia, which supports traumatised journalists; a member of the industry advisory panel to the federal government's Mindframe project on suicide and mental health, and works with the Federation of Ethnic Communities' Councils of Australia (FECCA).Professor Green has a background in the print news media, with experience as a daily newspaper editor. He holds a PhD in journalism from the University of Queensland, a Masters degree in Journalism and bachelor degrees in economics and arts.

Dr Sue Page teaches children's literature and creative writing at the University of South Australia. Her current research which has been published in Australia and overseas, examines how the Holocaust is represented to young people through fiction.

William (Bill) Park, CBE, AM, was a World War 2 infantry and signals soldier. He graduated with a Bachelor of Commerce in 1947 from the University of Queensland and spent the next fifty years in the business world. He served as chairman of the Brisbane Stock Exchange, president of the Brisbane Chamber of Commerce and a national vice president of the Institute of Directors. He was a member of Council of the Australian National University for thirteen years and also a Deputy Chairman and Councillor of the Kelvin Grove Council of Advanced Education. He is the patron of the Winston Churchill Memorial Trust and was awarded a CBE for services to business, and an AM for service to the community, finance and education. Before and since retirement he extensively researched his family history and more recently military history of WW2 with a special interest in the University of Queensland students of 1941 who served in the armed forces in that war. He graduated with a Master of Philosophy in 2009 from the School of Journalism and Communication, also from the University of Queensland.

Paul Skrebels is a Senior Lecturer in the School of Communication, International Studies and Languages at the Unversity of South Australia. A member of the Military Historical Society (SA branch), his research interests include war memoir and war fiction, the discourse of military history and military uniforms, insignia and equipment.

Dr Nigel Starck, a former journalist and television producer, teaches creative writing at the University of South Australia. His current project in the field of military history is a biography of the Australian prisoner-of-war author Russell Braddon (whose memoir *The Naked Island* has achieved sales of two million and, fifty-seven years after publication, remains in print).

Claire Woods is Professor of Communication and Writing in the School of Communication, International Studies and Languages, at the University of South Australia. She is teaching team leader in Professional Writing and Creative Communication and leader of the Narratives of War research group. She is co-editor with Judith Timoney of *Writings of War*, Lythrum Press, 2008. With support of an Army History Research Grant, she and Dr Paul Skrebels are currently revisiting the unit history of the 27th Battalion, AIF.

LYTHRVM

WWW.LYTHRUMPRESS.COM.AU